Mental Health
in
Organizations:
Personal Adjustment
and
Constructive Intervention

Mental Health in Organizations:

Personal Adjustment and Constructive Intervention

Erich P. Prien, Mark A. Jones,
Louise M. Miller, Robert Gulkin,
and Margaret Sutherland

Nelson-Hall nh Chicago

Library of Congress Cataloging in Publication Data
Main entry under title:

Mental health in organizations.

Bibliography: p.
Includes index.
1. Industrial psychiatry.   2. Adjustment (Psy-
chology)   I. Prien, Erich P., 1928–
RC967.5.M46   362.2   78-16757
ISBN O-88229-175-0

Manufactured in the United States of America

10 9 8 7 6 5 4 3 2 1

Contents

Preface

THE EXTENT OF the problem of personal adjustment in organizations is becoming increasingly apparent as evidenced by reports in the popular literature, newspapers, and magazines. The Federal government, through the office of the Secretary of Health, Education, and Welfare, provides additional testimony in a report entitled *Work in America*. The statistics of despair on job withdrawal, unresolved conflict, and more serious problems reflecting personal adjustment failure are, at the very least, appalling. Alcoholism, drug abuse, suicide, theft, and maladaptive behaviors are increasing in frequency. Whether this is an artifact of better record keeping or a reflection of a rise in the incidence is unknown, but the problems are enormous and demand attention.

Who should attend to these problems? Is the individual alone responsible for self-care? Must federal, state, or municipal governments intervene in the public interest? Are the employing organizations to be held accountable for the personal adjustment status of employees? Too many suffer too much for the nation to tolerate half solutions or, worse, a cavalier attitude toward relief.

Although behaviors indicative of personal adjustment failures result in significant economic costs for the organization, the costs to the individual are greater.

These individual costs are personal rather than economic and include: feelings of failure, meaninglessness, distress and alienation, loss of personal productivity, disintegration of personal relationships, and severe emotional and medical disorders.

Society's efforts to alleviate these various conditions have been less than successful. In fact, the history of the mental health professions is not distinguished by success in constructive intervention. At best, this approach has only salved the surface wound and has not solved the basic problem. There are too few professional man-hours available to continue this inefficient approach. Clearly a multiplier approach to intervention is called for—where the effort of one professional is multiplied through transfer of critical skills to nonprofessionals. Organization intervention strategies are needed, but unfortunately most are speculative, shotgun approaches. Also, the typical organization development interventionist is hired by management and is primarily concerned with the economic goals of the organization. Only passing attention is paid to the human needs of employees within the organization. What does seem to be a viable approach combines conventional organization development and job redesign. This is called the sociotechnical approach, and requires the highest order of professional skills.

Plan of the Book

The purpose of this book is to call attention to the relationship of the individual to the world of work. The current literature has emphasized negative outcomes of this relationship, specifically failures of personal adjustment. The other side of the coin is personal adjustment success which, for us, is of even greater importance. We intend to consider both the negative and the positive variables in developing a clearer picture of personal adjustment in organizations and in suggesting effective management methods.

The text is divided into two major sections, each comprised of four chapters. In Chapter One we present our concept of personal adjustment in organizations. In Chapter Two the link between the individual and the organization environment is specified and examined. In Chapter Three we examine the problems of measuring personal adjustment and present some of the pertinent research data concerning the organizational manifestations of personal adjustment. In Chapter Four the link between personal adjustment and the specific characteristics of the organization is developed. Taken as a unit, these four chapters provide the explanatory background for the second section which focuses on innovative management for human effectiveness. In Chapter Five the clinical model is examined. Included here is a short history of the attempts business and industry have made to define and to deal with the problem of mental health. In Chapter Six the concept and practice of organization development and its relationship to personal adjustment is explored. In Chapter Seven the sociotechnical approach is described and evaluated. We sum up and present in the final chapter a strategy of management and organization to optimize human effectiveness.

Numerous colleagues have read and commented on this book while in its various stages. Their suggestions for improving clarity have been incorporated and whatever errors or confusion remain must be attributed to the authors. Our special acknowledgement and appreciation to Donna Murphy and Vickie Cunningham who typed the manuscript.

Chapter 1

The Concept of Personal Adjustment

THE CONCEPTS OF mental health and personal adjustment typically conjure up images of utopian environments and conditions. A good personal adjustment, like motherhood and the flag, has intrinsic merit and is desirable in and of itself. No one would argue that a poor personal adjustment is a desirable or even tolerable condition. Yet, the statistics of adjustment failure indicate that these conditions exist in abundance and that, instead of decreasing in proportion to the increases in knowledge and technological developments in mental health, they are increasing at an alarming rate. Whether the recorded increases in adjustment failure are due to decrement in public mental health or to improved methods of gathering and reporting the statistical evidence is unknown. Whatever the causes, personal adjustment failure in its many forms is becoming recognized as a national problem. The consequences of personal adjustment failure in terms of the way individuals behave are of concern in both public and private organizations. These are the settings in which people function and, consequently, in which some of them malfunction.

Alcoholism, including drinking on and off the job, the use of drugs, theft, sabotage, and other critical behaviors are reaching epidemic proportions according to both the popular literature and the reports of managers. Less critical but still bothersome and costly are the hidden failures which do not have obvious symptoms in individual behavior. Dissatisfaction, negative spillover into the home life, and the deteriorating self-concept of workers have eventual outcomes, but are not necessarily related to the short-term economic state of the organization. For many people such as the poor, the underemployed, or the unemployed, the prevailing feelings are hopelessness, impotence, fear, mistrust, and general capitulation to the system. In some settings such as the public school system, specific provisions are made for constructive intervention. There, special education and resource teachers, counselors, and psychologists are employed to provide a helping service. Similarly there are many community agencies supported by public charitable donations or civic groups to which an individual might turn for assistance, if the individual has performed some self-diagnosis and is sufficiently motivated to improve the quality of his life. And, while these resources exist to provide help, those most in need appear to be those least likely to seek assistance.

In the private sector the "for profit" organization is far less likely to provide this type of constructive action facility since to do so would involve a substantial cost. This is usually viewed as an overhead cost and not necessarily a normal cost of doing business. Industrial executives surveyed to determine the goals of organizations typically rank profits first, with survival and/or growth of the business not far behind. Helping services for employee satisfaction or personal adjustment are ranked lower on the list in spite of the largesse of the individual executive or the corporation at "annual giving" time. Counseling or rehabilitation services provided by a few corporations are designed primarily to protect company investment, and are not the manifestation of a social consciousness. Obviously it is far more convenient to maintain a symptom oriented salvage operation than it is to design, construct and implement constructive intervention programs.

Attempts to link individual personal adjustment to the primary goals of the organization have not been very successful. In spite of the meager evidence, however, there is growing concern about organizational behaviors which can be interpreted as manifestations of personal adjustment failure. Now, research evidence linking work conditions, mental health, and the functioning of the organization is beginning to accumulate. Several studies show the impact of work itself on the employee's general personal adjustment. For example, Tannenbaum (1957) showed that there are measurable changes in personality traits of employees corresponding to changes in job design. In a later article Tannenbaum (1962) demonstrated considerably greater support of the impact of work changes on the individual employee as measured by satisfaction, productivity, and psychosomatic disorders. The most comprehensive study, performed by Kasl and French (1962), provided additional evidence relating variation in personal adjustment to job status and job level. Generally they found a higher incidence of psychosomatic complaints at the lower job levels. In addition, other indices indicate that employees in higher-level jobs have better personal adjustment on the average than those in lower-level jobs. The results presented in this study, which was conducted in two companies, each with over .

10,000 employees, are quite convincing although the authors point out that the true causal relations are unknown.

Kornhauser (1965) produced a definitive study by investigating the mental health of industrial workers in the Detroit area. In this study an elaborate interview questionnaire was designed to obtain measures of operationally defined facets of personal adjustment. The most striking finding was that personal adjustment varied directly and consistently with the level of job difficulty. This supported the results presented by Kasl and French, although Kornhauser probed for causes on a broader scale. Employees with better personal adjustment are distinguishably different from those having poorer personal adjustment in degree of anxiety, feelings of self-esteem, expressed hostility, sociability, and life satisfaction. In part these symptoms are consequences of the individuals' personal adjustment status. These symptoms may also have implications for the individuals' off-the-job life.

In a subsequent study Levinson, Price, Munden, Mandle, and Solley (1966) provide evidence consistent with that presented by Kornhauser. These researchers used a similar approach but studied employees of a public utility firm located in a community smaller than in Kornhauser's work. Despite the dissimilar settings, the general conclusions are markedly similar: individual personal adjustment is complexly associated with the characteristics of the job and of the work setting.

The research evidence summarized in the preceding paragraphs seems sufficient to support the notion of a relationship between individual personal adjustment and job characteristics including the conditions which exist within business and industrial organizations. While the exact causal relations may not have been clearly established in these studies, it appears justifiable to conclude that the individual's personal adjustment status is affected by the job, the job status, and the conditions of work. It is also conceivable that poor personal adjustment results in an individual's ability to retain only a low-level job. These relationships, when combined with the fact that well over sixty million people are regularly employed in some organizational setting, justify a substantial concern for the personal adjustment of employees in organizations.

Personal adjustment is a definable and measurable characteristic which has been studied extensively. A thorough understanding of the concept and of the conditions leading to both good and poor personal adjustment are essential before effective constructive action can be considered. In other words, we must understand the problem before we can begin to develop constructive solutions. The book's intended audience includes both our professional colleagues and the managers and executives who can make the decision to take constructive actions.

Personal Adjustment

Definitions of personal adjustment by clinical and counseling psychologists typically emphasize pathological behavior—bizarre behaviors readily distinguishable from normal behavior even by the relatively uninformed layman. Uncontrollable rage, immobilizing depression, acts of self-destruction, and wildly distorted beliefs are unmistakable manifestations of a complete personal adjustment failure. However, relatively little emphasis has been placed on the concept of the normal personality and the variations in personal adjustment which are still within the normal range. This "normal" variability is sometimes sufficient to cause an individual considerable discomfort, possibly anguish and despair, and *may* lead to more serious and disabling pathology. While it has been estimated that one in ten individuals in this country will be touched by mental illness some time in their lives, there are no readily available estimates of the proportion of the population directly or indirectly affected by personal adjustment failures. It might not be unrealistic to assume that 100 percent of the population will experience some meaningful contact with personal adjustment failure or incidences of personal incompetence. Obviously our consideration is not limited to bizarre behaviors, but includes everyday phenomena such as escapism through the use of drugs or alcohol, prolonged feelings of personal discomfort, or worry and anxiety which may hinder, but not totally disable, the individual. On this basis it appears necessary to formulate a definition of individual personal adjustment as follows:

> From the viewpoint of the individual, personal adjustment is determined by the degree of congruence between his requirements and his realizations including all physiological, cognitive, and affective elements in his total life space.

Obviously this definition is very restrictive, with no reference to social norms. The emphasis is upon satisfaction of needs as defined by the individual for himself. For example, one of the requirements of an aged recluse is isolation from other people. A requirement of a teenage delinquent might be the excitement experienced driving a stolen car. Thus, this definition of individual personal adjustment is theoretical and stripped of all the complexities created by a cultural value system. In the pragmatic sense this definition does not provide a very convenient basis for measuring behaviors which reflect personal adjustment within organizations. In both research and practice, measurement of personal adjustment along a good-poor continuum is essential. Normally, to obtain data concerning requirements and realizations an observer must interrogate the individual. An alternate approach is to witness actual behaviors and infer the existence of the individual's requirements and realizations. Since the definition includes physiological, cognitive, and affective elements, this kind of measurement (when the individual is aware he is being observed or measured) constitutes a very significant element in the individual's total life space. A more practical observer-oriented definition which lends itself to measurement is as follows:

> From the viewpoint of an observer, personal adjustment is the evaluation of congruence of an individual's behavior with various societally ascribed role requirements.

This definition refers to both other people and institutions with which the individual has either a direct or indirect relationship. These relationships in the form of role requirements may vary for an individual on a day-to-day basis, and will incorporate the standards to which the individual responds. Since most individuals have several roles (worker, husband, neighbor), the evaluation of personal adjustment is made by various observers. And, as we will point out in a later chapter, these evaluations will be based in part on the values of the observer. Specifically, the behaviors which represent positive personal adjustment to one observer may represent the opposite to another, based on different observer values. The personal adjustment of a rebellious industrial worker may be evaluated negatively by a foreman whose values are based in part on production quotas. The same individual may be seen as having good personal adjustment by a labor union organizer whose values are based on the accomplishment of other goals. The evaluation of personal adjustment is then not universal. Evaluation is an observer judgment and each one can be correct within the unique value system.

Recognizing that a value judgment is involved in categorizing an individual's personal adjustment as good or poor, the problem of identification of contributing factors remains. The wording of the above definition leads to a criterion statement and the possible specification of the measures which will represent variation in personal adjustment. In the case of both the individual-oriented and the observer-oriented definition, variation in personal adjustment can be measured. We can specify the behaviors which reflect the personal adjustment continuum and then place individuals at points where their behavior corresponds to that level of adjustment. In this procedure it is possible to become too specific. Even the individual with optimal personal adjustment experiences moments of failure. An individual may experience a moment of maladjustment as a result of transient conditions or circumstances. For example, when an individual is startled and is unable to identify the source of his alarm he may experience very substantial discomfort. An hour later he may experience quite the opposite and enjoy near-optimal personal adjustment when requirements and experience correspond. In evaluating an individual's personal adjustment, then, we are concerned with an average obtained over prolonged periods of time. Periodic evaluation can conceivably be made at weekly or monthly intervals depending on conditions. This derivation of the measurement and evaluation of personal adjustment is consistent with the concept of homeostasis—a status of equilibrium is optimum. That is, an individual's personal adjustment will vary as requirements change but repeated measurement over a period of time will yield an average level.

Motivation for Adjustment

Theories of personality include the concept of motivation as a way of explaining why individuals behave in a particular way. Individual differences in motivation are accepted and commonly used to explain differences in behavior. Thus, we can explain individual efforts to improve adjustment only by viewing motivation as the force which gets a person from state A to state B. Motivation in general gives magnitude or intensity as well as direction to behavior. This is reflected in statements about an individual such as "He left no stone unturned to make money." Obviously, the behavior has direction (making money) and intensity (no stone unturned) that have meaning as descriptions of human behavior. Two theories of motivation have some relevance to our general area of inquiry if only because they have been incorporated in industrial-organizational psychology theories.

Helen Peak (1955) views attitudes as either dependent or independent variables in relation to motivation. Peak introduces the idea of instrumentality: behavior is useful in obtaining some end. The assumption here is that an attitude toward an object is related to the consequences of obtaining or not obtaining that object. The behavior which is instrumental in obtaining the object acquires a positive affect (reinforcement or satisfaction). If repeated with sufficient frequency this link will stabilize. The expectation of satisfaction produces behavior of a specific type. Thus, the individual who works harder receives a higher rate of pay, and this in turn provides the means to improve the quality of life. In addition, Peak includes choice and intensity as properties of the motive construct. Thus, according to Peak and as refined by Vroom (1965), individuals behave because they expect their acts will be instrumental in achieving a consequence of positive value. While there has been no effort to formulate a comprehensive theory other than one which links attitudes and behavior, the concept of personal adjustment in organizations incorporates measures of the individual's satisfaction with his job. In our view, satisfaction, and particularly increasing satisfaction, is an indicator of good personal adjustment. Thus, individual efforts to increase satisfaction provide the basis for our position that personal adjustment has a positive value to the individual and that motivation can be directed toward improving personal adjustment.

The second and more general theory is by White (1959) who proposed that the then current theories were inadequate to explain the necessary conditions for activity and/or learning. To overcome this deficiency he defines competence as the fitness or the ability of the individual to carry on transactions with the environment which result in his maintenance, growth, and prosperity. Specifically, White proposes that manipulative drives provoke exploratory activity. When these activities lead to satisfaction in goal accomplishment the individual experiences feelings of *efficacy*. Since these drives are not physiological, White postulates an effective competence motive. In other words, an individual will strive to be effective (given the opportunity), and when he is effective will realize positive reinforcement. What is important here is that White views the development of competence as critical to the individual's personal adjustment. The concepts provided by White have been elaborated by Brayfield (1965) as partial support for his argument that the principal objective of psychology as a practical endeavor is enhancing human effectiveness. In combining the theories of Peak, White, and Brayfield, the purposeful intervention by psychologists (or, for that matter, organization management) should focus on helping individuals achieve competence and thus better personal adjustment. For one individual these feelings of competence may stem from earning more money, while for another the critical success might be achieving expertise in his craft. Constructive action then must provide individuals with opportunities to grow and to flourish within their work environment or, if nothing more, must remove obstacles to individual growth and development. More will be said in subsequent chapters about the obstacles which are embedded in management philosophy and in the process of managing organizations.

Chapter 2

Personal Adjustment in the Work Setting

THE OBSERVER-ORIENTED definition of personal adjustment stated in Chapter One represents a person-by-situation interaction in which both the characteristics of the individual and the characteristics of the situation must be considered. This conceptual framework is not new and has been described elsewhere in the literature using various terminology and different objectives. Perhaps the most refined treatment of this concept is in mental measurement in which the objective is the precise measurement of individual psychological characteristics. Cronbach (1970) specifically accounts for the individual-situation interaction in terms of treatment · effects or stability of test scores over occasions. Translated to fit the needs of this book, Cronbach's treatment effects recognize that individuals do behave differently depending on the nature of the setting. Thus, measurements taken in different situations will include the effect of those situations. In the field of psychological testing, the effects of situational differences are treated as errors which vary from one situation to another. Other authors such as Fredrickson (1972) and Sells (1963) focus on the specific effect of different situational characteristics on individual behavior. Sells, particularly in drawing on interaction theory, takes the position that differences in behavior are not accounted for by either inner or outer forces separately but by their interaction. Thus, complete understanding of individual behavior, which includes personal adjustment, requires understanding both individual psychological characteristics and the characteristics of the situation in which the individual must function. In a pragmatic treatment of this concept, Pervin (1968) takes the position that performance and satisfaction as general psychological states are determined by individual/environment fit. Thus, high correspondence between the individual and the environment results in relatively high performance and satisfaction, while low correspondence produces a low level of individual performance and satisfaction.

If we combine these ideas it becomes apparent that a better understanding of personal adjustment requires identifying the effects of unique situation characteristics. For example, what are the effects on personal adjustment of situation characteristics such as the size of the work group, physical distance between workers, leadership style, repetitiveness of tasks, and so on? While an infinite number of these specific characteristics can be identified, effective research requires some organization, such as the taxonomy of organization characteristics proposed by Sells (1963).

The point is clear that human behavior is complexly related to many variables which lie in several domains. A domain is simply a category of specific variables that share something in common. For our purpose these domains are individual characteristics (e.g., abilities, aptitudes, personality characteristics, and interests) and one or more situational characteristics. One example is work group characteristics; another is the organizational characteristics of structure and climate. What becomes important to understand personal adjustment is information from studies which simultaneously investigate human behavior in various settings or, in our case, across domains. For example, we might seek to learn when personal adjustment is best—at the beginning of the week, during the middle of the week, or at the end of the week, with all other factors held constant. From information appearing in the popular media it would seem that personal adjustment in the work setting is lowest on Friday or Monday and reaches a peak during the middle weekdays. This is based on reports that absenteeism on Fridays and Mondays reaches 15 percent and is lower during midweek. If we accept absenteeism, a form of job aversion, as a criterion of personal adjustment, then this conclusion would be logical. On the surface this example may be oversimplified, and closer examination may show that the workers who are absent on Monday are not absent on Friday. This might suggest that the two groups are absent for different reasons: the worker absent on Monday may be avoiding a work situation which is threatening and aversive; whereas the worker absent on Friday may have reached his limit of toleration. Still closer examination requires measurement of conditions within the work setting. We may find that workers are absent on Friday not simply because they have reached their endurance limit, but because pressure from management to meet quotas increases systematically throughout the week. The conditions resulting from this pressure may include speeded-up production lines, more demanding supervision, or less tolerance of errors. Thus, these are the conditions which might result in individual-environment misfit and consequently produce job aversion.

While the rationale of this concept is perfectly logical, there are relatively few investigations of human behavior in relation to the characteristics of the situation in which that behavior occurs. It appears that the problem is even more basic. Very limited research has been conducted which would provide the basis for describing differences in situation characteristics. While descriptive schemes have been offered, they are based primarily on theoretical analyses rather than systematic empirical investigations.

The environment in which the individual functions not only influences behavior, but also may influence more enduring personality characteristics. While personality change has been a subject of concern, the magnitude of change of the more enduring personality characteristics has been underestimated in the past. Kelly (1955) studied personality change over twenty years and found that while the essential structure remains intact, there are measurable changes generally attributed to maturation. Only recently has this nebulous situation been given more systematic attention. Mischel (1969) argues that while behavioral dispositions in terms of traits or psychodynamic theory are relatively stable, actual behavior will vary depending on situational conditions. What the individual does is contingent upon not only his personality but also all the other elements of his point-in-time life space. What appear to be inconsistencies in behavior may not be at all. In fact, the situation (life space) may require accommodation—and thus atypical behavior—for prolonged periods. This, in turn, may lead to permanent change from what previously had been considered relatively permanent, enduring personality characteristics. Unfortunately this does not define which aspects of the situation are potent or, further, which aspects of personality or behavior are affected by these situational characteristics. The conclusive answers to such questions as, "Does long-term exposure to a particular condition lead to permanent change in basic personality characteristics?" will require very extensive studies of the type and design proposed by Fredrickson (1972). This research includes case studies of individuals across a sampling of situations.

From the viewpoint of the individual, the world of work is a relevant segment of his psychological life space and ecological environment. These terms are not arbitrarily selected; both have specific meanings. Psychological life space consists of elements or conditions to which the individual may respond in daily life. These conditions are constantly changing and require an adaptive response by the individual. The ecological environment, on the other hand, includes the totality of both changing and stable characteristics.

Psychological Life Space

The psychological life space of a worker consists of interpersonal transactions with coworkers, the job itself, and the immediate work environment.

As established earlier, the elementary link exists between job satisfaction and the elements of the psychological life space. For example, the research on leadership and supervision documents the importance of interpersonal transactions in job satisfaction, but the specifics of the relationship are unknown.

An extensive review of the research literature by Herzberg et al. (1957) concluded that job satisfaction is further linked to individual performance and production. Because any factors which influence productivity in the industrial setting can be immediately translated into organization profits and survival, the implications of this relationship are of interest to the pragmatic businessman.

The propositions which emerge from the theoretical stand taken by Herzberg are more specific to our interest; job satisfaction is linked to mental health of the industrial worker. While this may have been a matter of conjecture in the past, the work of Kasl and French (1962), Walker and Guest (1952), Levinson et al. (1966), and Kornhauser (1965) quite eloquently plead the case of the industrial worker. These studies, each comprehensive in nature, very dramatically point out the impacts of technology, industrial mechanization, fractionation of jobs, and job design on the personal adjustment of the in-

dustrial worker. The consequences are not limited to behavior in the work setting but, as Kornhauser points out,
there are effects in other segments of the individual's life
space. As described by Kornhauser the deleterious effects
of the job and work situation can be and often are manifest in the individual's adjustment within his family. Further, these effects may have an impact, direct or indirect,
on the personal adjustment of other family members.

In industrial organizations, work and work situations are under the control of parties concerned with improving economic performance and efficiency but often
without the social-personal consequences of their decisions. For the most part, economic factors dictate how
the business will be conducted with, at best, secondary
concern for the human condition. Bass (1952) very
cogently argued for a more comprehensive business viewpoint to include economic *and* social and personal responsibility. Social responsibility concerns the implications of
management of the enterprise for the public interests;
personal responsibility concerns the implications for
employees. Obviously, an enterprise must survive if it is
to serve the interest of the public at large and the
employees. (We might argue that there are some industries or organizations which might better cease to exist.)
Management must somehow be responsible to the
various interested parties simultaneously, and make the
appropriate trade-off decisions. When a decision will
utilize technological innovation but will have detrimental
effects on employee satisfaction, the increased profits
which might result from use of the technology must be
weighed against the human costs. Obviously, if it is a
question of survival, then the economic concerns will
usually be paramount. For example, it is illegal today to
trade employee physical health for increased profits by
not installing costly noise abatement devices. There are,
on the other hand, no laws requiring industry to train
supervisors appropriately or to design jobs which will
enhance or, at the very least, not detract from the
worker's personal adjustment.

The Ecological Environment

Barker (1968) differentiates between ecological environment and psychological life space by defining the former in terms of the relatively permanent characteristics with which the individual has contact. Only some of these characteristics are relevant to the individual while others may never be relevant, at least in affecting his behavior. Barker includes in his scheme such characteristics as the prevailing temperature in the geographic locality, the number of organizational entities with which the individual might interact in the community, the size of the community in which the individual resides, the degree of industrialization, and even the physical space and architecture of settings in which the individual lives.

While Barker's theoretical concept may help explain variation in individual behavior in terms of the individual's interaction with his environment, little research is directed toward understanding the industrial worker's personal adjustment. Obviously, this broad, cross-domain approach to the study of individual behavior has considerable potential, making this void in the research literature all the more apparent.

Personal Adjustment and Organization Variables

A substantial amount of research has been conducted which supports the relation of organization structure and climate to personal adjustment. In this research the focus is individual and group performance effectiveness which includes absenteeism, turnover, and other behaviors indicative of poor personal adjustment. The most conclusive positions are those resulting from reviews of the research literature by Porter and Lawler (1965) and Forehand and Gilmer (1964). The main conclusion of both reviews is that there are obvious relationships between organization characteristics and individual and group performances, but the diversity of research methodologies, variables, and research objectives makes cross-study evaluations extremely difficult. While one study may show a relationship between an organization characteristic and an individual behavior, other studies may fail to replicate the finding. One relationship which has been demonstrated with sufficient frequency to support a general conclusion is that job withdrawal does increase in proportion to work group size. The exact nature of the causal relationship remains unknown since there are several variable concomitants of work group size such as degree of task specialization, access to supervisor, physical proximity to other workers, and the characteristics of the work. Unfortunately, studies have not been sufficiently precise to specifically identify the causal relationships, nor do these reports provide detailed descriptions of the nature and characteristics of the setting.

Work under the rubric of action research has linked organizational climate to individual behavior. The most convincing studies performed in industrial settings are those by Litwin and Stringer (1968) and Meyer (in Tagiuri and Litwin, 1968), all of whom used individual employee perception of organization climate as the main experimental variable. These studies, to be treated in detail later, indicate that the individual's perception of such things as the reward system, existence and maintenance of performance standards, plus other climate characteristics is related to both feelings of satisfaction and specific behaviors.

The work performed in educational settings relating characteristics of organization climate to student behavior demonstrates the relationship between student satisfaction and student performance and perception of organization climate (Pervin, 1968). However, Pervin also underscores a critical unanswered question: Is it the actual organization or the perceived organization which bears a causal relation to behavior? This same question has been raised by Berdie (1967) who collected objective data describing organizations and student perceptions of these same organizations. The results of his study show virtually no overlap between the objective characteristics of organizations and the perceived characteristics.

Overall, many studies conducted in industrial organizations and academic settings provide results consistent with the position taken in this book—that complete understanding of individual behavior requires understanding of the setting in which that behavior occurs. The main unresolved questions concern the appropriate approach to the measurement of organization characteristics and the derivation of taxonomies of organization level characteristics to be used in further research. Only when these two questions are answered will we begin to accumulate the information necessary to support constructive intervention.

In terms of the focus of this book relatively few studies have been reported which would clearly substantiate our position which links both individual and situation variables to personal adjustment. In fact, our position must be supported by inference and speculation from a few key studies and a variety of tangentially related studies. The studies concerned specifically with an industrial worker's mental health use such criteria of personal adjustment failure as job withdrawal or aberrant behavior (i.e., drug usage, alcoholism, sabotage, and interpersonal conflict) within the work situation. In our analysis we will also take liberties in drawing on more remotely related studies which describe the phenomena or which document the general potency of environmental characteristics as determinants of human behavior.

Chapter 3

Measuring Personal Adjustment

THE THEORETICAL DEFINITIONS of personal adjustment developed in Chapter One are necessary but not sufficient for practical concerns. Their two fundamental problems are immediately evident: the accurate diagnosis of personal adjustment and the prescription of appropriate remedial intervention.

The effectiveness of mental health practitioners is determined by various complex elements of which assessment/diagnosis and intervention are only two. However, the pivotal element is assessment. Inaccurate assessment fails to identify the maladjusted individual; inaccurate diagnosis fails to specify the etiology and/or dynamics of personal adjustment failure. Since personal adjustment by our definition is complexly determined, the diagnostic technique must yield sufficient information both to establish the relative or normative level of adjustment *and* to specify the salient elements contributing to that adjustment level for the individual.

Ideally, a *direct* measure of both level and dynamics of personal adjustment would be desirable. Unfortunately, as with all psychological states or processes, direct measurement is impossible. Only what an individual does is subject to observation and measurement, and those observed behaviors are then the basis for inferring the psychological state or process. Therefore, the person who *behaves* erratically or abnormally is maladjusted by inference. Inference should be empirically verified but, in practice, the validation research has not been very encouraging.

One approach to increasing the accuracy or validity of the inference process is by carefully specifying the criteria of personal adjustment. A conceptual criterion as defined by Astin "is a verbal statement of important or socially relevent outcomes based on the more general purposes or aims of the sponsor."[1] The conceptual criterion then provides the basis for specific statements of criterion behaviors which are subject to observation or which produce a retrievable trace record.

Several composites of personal adjustment criteria have been suggested by psychologists. Hoppock (1957) proposes a measure based on earnings, percentage of time employed, health, satisfaction in human relations, and job satisfaction. He bases this formula on the notion that an individual with a stable income at least has the opportunity to survive until a spontaneous recovery occurs. Glatter (1957) takes issue with Hoppock's economic criterion, but does agree on two of the five criteria Hoppock offers: satisfaction in human relations and job satisfaction. He adds the concepts of self-actualization, awareness, and happiness which lean heavily on

---

[1]A. Astin, "Criterion Centered Research," *Educational and Psychological Measurement* 24 (1964): 809.

humanitarian values. Glatter comes closer to defining a conceptual criterion than does Hoppock who apparently was more concerned with observability and measurement than with the concept itself. However, Lanyon, in discussing mental health systems, begins in a vein similar to Hoppock:

> It is common knowledge that a major factor in improving the living standards of any society is an increase in productivity, the amount of useful work performed per worker.[2]

The obvious extension of this cliché to personal adjustment of industrial workers is that the objective of intervention is basically an economic gain.

Any definition of a conceptual criterion of personal adjustment will have its proponents and critics. At this point in the development of professional psychology, the Zeitgeist appears to demand something more than economically oriented criteria. One argument is that there are several parties at interest to the mental health of American workers. In view of these multiple interests a conceptual criterion of personal adjustment requires social and personal considerations in addition to traditional economic ones.

As defined in Chapter One personal adjustment is not limited to economic concerns. It is the evaluation of congruence of an individual's behavior with various societally ascribed role requirements. Thus, the conceptual criterion statement describes all relevant outcomes to the various parties-at-interest. It is the degree of congruence (or the reverse, the sum of the discrepancies) between an individual's behavior and the various role requirements. In this way we provide the basis for measuring personal adjustment. The practical problem, then, is to identify the behaviors which are *valid* signs of good or poor personal adjustment in organizations.

---

[2]I. S. Lanyon, "Mental Health Technology," *American Psychologist* 26 (1971): 1071.

Measurement and Inference

As with any psychological variable, it is not possible to obtain a direct measure of a construct such as personal adjustment. Thus, to assess an individual's adjustment and to specify to some extent the etiology of an individual's state of adjustment, it is necessary to infer from observable behavior. This process of inference then begins with observation of, for example, occurrences of interpersonal conflict, excessive use of alcohol, drug use, personal dispensary visits, absences, or a self-report on degree of job satisfaction/dissatisfaction. While the validity of these behaviors as signs of personal adjustment may be questioned, this formula provides the basis for empirical research.

Ideally, the reliability of each measure should be demonstrated so that it becomes possible to attribute the behavior with some degree of confidence to individual differences rather than to occasional situational factors. In other words, if absence serves as one measure of personal adjustment, a consistent or statistically reliable pattern of absences would have different meaning and implications than a single absence during a local flu epidemic. However, when considering our proposed definition of personal adjustment it is clear that transient conditions may contribute to and result in poor adjustment. Since these conditions are temporary and often of short duration, the paradox becomes apparent; measures of behaviors which may be a function of poor adjustment cannot be demonstrated as reliable because of the transient nature of the situation. Only when an individual is consistently affected by transient situations will he or she become identified as having an adjustment problem. Therefore, in pragmatic terms, poor adjustment cannot be reliably inferred from isolated instances, and thus probably should be ignored in measurement.

Returning to inference, at best we can only demonstrate a degree of probability when we say, "If a person is absent often, or if he visits the dispensary frequently, or if he expresses gross job dissatisfaction, then he is poorly adjusted." In other words, there is some probability that frequency of plant dispensary visits, for example, is a function of personal adjustment and thus a proper index or measure. It becomes the task of research to establish and confirm that level of probability to increase confidence in the inference process itself and to provide a basis for valid prediction and constructive intervention.

At a more pragmatic level, one well-documented problem exists which threatens confidence in the inferential process. Research indicates that judgmental strategies may vary radically depending on the perceptual dispositions of the observer. For example, one observer might perceive absenteeism as antiorganizational behavior while another views it as a manifestation of poor personal adjustment. Their different perceptions would probably result in the collection of different types of data or at least different interpretations of the same data.

Another problem stemming from the measurement of behavior is that some methods may be technically superior to others. For instance, trace measures such as data drawn from records have the advantage of being unobtrusive and therefore less subject to experimenter effects. On the other hand, direct observations may prove more relevant or valid. This, again, is a question to be investigated by research, but each method has its own merits depending on circumstances.

Although caution is obviously required when making inferences from behavioral measurements, it is a necessary and acceptable process in psychology. When measures can be demonstrated as reliable and the probability of accurate inference established by such means as validation, we are justified in having confidence in inference.

Criterion Measures of Personal Adjustment

Research on employee behavior has been very extensive although the objectives only infrequently include increased understanding of personal adjustment. These behaviors cover a wide spectrum, but in terms of the assessment of personal adjustment the following classification is convenient: (1) withdrawal behaviors (absenteeism, turnover); (2) reactive behaviors (slowdown, sabotage); (3) those consequences where the individual is the only one to lose or suffer (depression, psychosomatic ailments); and (4) job attitudes (job dissatisfaction, morale). While the behaviors symptomatic of personal adjustment failure are commonly viewed as if the individual were accountable, our position is the opposite. We are convinced that situation characteristics contribute to these failures, and thus the organization must share in the accountability. To substantiate our position it is first necessary to delineate the criterion measures of personal adjustment in the work setting.

Job Withdrawal

Personal adjustment is complex and measurement might focus on any one or several manifestations. However, most of the research has dealt with the consequences of adjustment *failure* since these are the more troublesome. Many of these investigations have been subjective or evaluative, and thus it would be a formidable task to integrate them into a scheme acceptable to everyone. One means of minimizing this confusion is to view personal adjustment in terms of statistical occurrence of certain behaviors which can reflect the level of adjustment. This approach tends to be more objective, at least on the surface, and also more parsimonious.

The most obvious and least investigated withdrawal behaviors are daydreaming, frequent coffee breaks, intraoffice chattering, and inordinate numbers of trips to the restroom. The employee may utilize such means to cope with transient situations in the work setting. A third-year lineman apprentice for a midwestern utility company thinks the coffee break is a good deal because "You've got to have a little fun on the job, see . . . I think things like that make for good working conditions."[3] Unfortunately there are no figures to substantiate the assertion that such behaviors are means of dealing with unpleasant aspects of the job. To date, no one has kept such close tabs on employees to ascertain the amount of time consumed by coffee breaks and such.

Another extensively used form of job withdrawal is the dispensary visit for a somatic complaint. These maladies are interpreted as reflecting, with some sensitivity, the stress of a job. French (1962) states that poor mental health shows a positive correlation with the tendency to seek medical aid and report physical symptoms. According to W. J. Fulton (1949), less than 50 percent of the patients seen by medical departments are found to have physical causes for their complaints. Further, according to his findings, 85 percent of direct medical services are utilized by only 30 percent of the employees. Levinson (1964) studied more than 3,400 actively employed men and women of the New York Telephone Company. He reports that 25 percent of these employees accounted for more than half of all episodes of disability, approximately two-thirds of all days of disability, and a similar proportion of sickness. This same group also exhibited more different kinds of illnesses, more mood and behavior disturbances, and were more frequently involved in administrative conflicts. From these figures there is substantial evidence to indicate that a significant percentage of workers experience psychosomatic disorders within the work setting.

The frequency of dispensary visits as a measure has received little attention although frequency of psychosomatic complaints has been recognized and was included by Kornhauser (1965). Tan (1972) used measures

---

[3]H. Levinson et al., *Men, Management, and Mental Health* (Cambridge, Mass.: Harvard University Press, 1966), p. 73.

of both personal and job-related dispensary visits and found the two measures highly correlated. However, the relationship of these two measures to absenteeism was not uniform. White employees who were absent more frequently used the dispensary more often, but this relationship did not appear for black employees. Similarly, Ronan and Prien (1973) found that absenteeism, tardiness, and dispensary visits were differentially related depending on job level. For example, absenteeism and dispensary visits were related for factory employees, but were not related for technical and professional employees.

Although no statistics are available, there is reason to suspect that tardiness also mirrors to some extent the same motivation as absenteeism. One can assume that a percentage of tardiness is attributed to some aversive characteristics of the work setting.

Absenteeism is probably the most troublesome form of job withdrawal because of economic implications and the relative impotence of industrial management to deal constructively with the phenomenon. According to the 1954 survey of mental health in industry conducted by the Menninger Foundation, only 5 percent of sickness–absenteeism was due to on-the-job causes such as injury. Serrin, reporting on the assembly lines of the Detroit automobile factories, states that "absenteeism, which traditionally ran at a rate of about 2.5 percent of the work force, has soared in the past five years to more than 5.5 percent, an all-time high."[4] Earl Bramblett, a General Motors vice-president for personnel, elaborated by asserting that on Fridays and Mondays "it's not wild to have 10 percent of the people absent."[5]

Absenteeism has long been recognized as a researchable phenomenon and a considerable body of data

---

[4]W. Serrin, "The Assembly Line," *The Atlantic* 228 (1971): 66.

[5]*Ibid.*

has been accumulated to substantiate several general conclusions. These conclusions are: (1) absenteeism is a measurable individual difference characteristic; (2) absenteeism is an outcome of individual situation transaction; (3) absenteeism is a modifiable behavior although the exact causes vary depending on the situation and the individuals involved; and (4) absenteeism has been linked to other behaviors suggesting a more general syndrome, that of job withdrawal.

During recent years increasing attention has been given to withdrawal linked to the abusive use of alcohol and drugs. Although the eventual consequence might be limited to the individual, there are also organizational consequences *while* the individual remains employed. One such consequence is absenteeism but it is not possible to divide the incidence of alcoholism from the mainstream of absenteeism statistics. Habbe (1968) reports one estimate by the National Council on Alcoholism which posits 5 percent of all employees as problem drinkers. Those alcoholics who cause their companies the greatest losses are fairly long-service employees in the 35–50 year age range. In that report it is estimated that alcoholism is causing American industries a $7.5 billion annual loss.

While management actions to cope with some of these withdrawal behaviors will be discussed later in detail, one observation is warranted here. Reports of the statistics of despair are abundant, but reports of successful constructive action are few. For example, one approach has been to institute absenteeism control policies in the coercive sense. Employees who accrue a set number of unexcused absences during a stated time period are fired. Thus, while the incidences of absenteeism remain within manageable proportions, the true problem remains unsolved and perhaps invisible. Withdrawal is a person/environment product, and intervention by coercive control or employee selection is nothing more than a "head in the sand" solution.

Reactive Behaviors

Reactive behaviors differ from withdrawal behaviors primarily in terms of individual adjustment styles. Thus, two individuals in exactly the same setting might experience the identical degree of stress, but behave quite differently. One avoids the situation; the other fights. Why people choose different strategies is unknown.

One of the subtler forms of reactive behavior, albeit one which could be quite costly for a company, is restriction of output. Even before World War I Max Weber commented that the worker's outlook and the state of his relations with his employer have an important effect upon output. After studying large-scale German industry, he was led to emphasize the phenomenon of slowdown, or the intentional restriction of output, apparent even in the absence of an organized union (Sheppard, 1955). One example of restriction of output in a canning plant is described by Mathewson (Sheppard, 1955). He found that the workers threw pieces of tinplate into the machines or incorrectly placed the tins to retard the conveyor belt, which had been speeded up by the management.

Mathewson's example reveals not only restriction of output but sabotage as well. As Serrin (1971) points out, discontent shown through vandalism is more obvious to organizations than a slowdown.

Theft also reflects the reactive phenomenon in the world of work. Zeitlin states that "... employees in American business steal between 8.5 and 10 billion dollars a year. About four billion of this total is theft of cash and merchandise from retail establishments. The remainder is lost through kickbacks, bribery, theft of time, and loss of corporate secrets."[6] Over 75 percent of all employees engage in some form of merchandise shrinkage. Further, a store's own workers steal three times as much as do shoplifters.

---

[6]L. R. Zeitlin, "A Little Larceny Can Do a Lot for Employee Morale," *Psychology Today* 5 (1971): 22.

The most blatant reactive behavior employed by workers to express their grievances is the organized strike. According to the 1969 Department of Labor figures, there were 5,700 work stoppages with an average duration of 22.5 days. These stoppages involved 2.4 million workers or 3.5 percent of the total employed work force. These stoppages resulting from labor/management disputes resulted in 42.8 million idle mandays during 1969, or 17.3 idle mandays per worker involved.

In 1971 the issues underlying the reaction of employees at the General Motors Vega plant concerned the work, the conditions of work, and management philosophy. Newspaper and magazine accounts and TV documentaries stressed that employee grievances concerned meaningless, repetitive work, the impersonal and inconsiderate position of management, and *did not* include reference to the tangibles (pay, hours of work, vacation, benefits, and so on) typically found in past labor/management conflicts. Why this long overdue shift in employee grievances occurred remains unknown. Perhaps workers themselves are coming to grips with the basic questions about the meaning and the value of work.

From this limited review it can be seen that employees have at their disposal numerous and varied means of reacting to what they find in the work setting. But while the figures presented here are as accurate as possible, the inferences are made in accordance with the value system of the observer. We have interpreted these statistics as evidence of the potential detrimental effects of some of the conditions of work on the workers' personal adjustment.

Individual Consequences

Both forms of behaviors—withdrawal and reaction—have definite economic consequences for the organization. In contrast, individual consequences such as morale, alienation, ulcers, hypertension, and so on are typically not publicly observable behaviors. Their economic costs to the organization are indirect and are either ignored or are treated mechanically through health and accident policies or in company medical facilities. Individual consequences may be conveniently classified as either the affective functioning of the individual, or bodily or somatic expression of internal states.

Ignoring the more severe clinical expressions of affective dysfunction (e.g., neurosis, psychosis) there are numerous other emotional responses to states of psychological tension or stress which occur with great frequency among industrial workers. The positive affective states of the phenomena include feelings of accomplishment, happiness, positive morale as a generalized feeling of well- being, and the multitude of nebulous states of mind that people label as desirable. In contrast are the feelings of alienation, depression, discouragement, and failure. In general, the negative states seem to reflect an inability to cope with one's environment. The immediate consequences of these feelings are the lack of comfort of the individual and perhaps lower effectiveness.

The second category includes those internal states which are manifest through bodily expression. The most common expression is the psychosomatic disorder. In this condition, a fairly long-standing state of tension results in actual organic damage to some body system, although the individual need not be aware of the existence of tension. However, lacking any means of expression, the prolonged state of emotional tension appears to precipitate bodily malfunction. The classic example is the gastric ulcer, but such effects are not limited to the digestive tract and may occur almost anywhere (e.g., skin, respiratory system, endocrine system, and so on).

One final area in which negative feelings may be expressed is in an individual's interpersonal behavior. Given that certain states entail some degree of psychological tension, one's interactions with others may serve as a mode of tension release. For example, Dollard and Miller (1950) suggest that tension resulting from frustration tends to produce aggressive behavior or "free floating hostility." This tension, in turn, is released by directing aggression at others.

The unifying characteristic of the individual consequences is their essentially private nature. The individual knows what is being experienced, but may not be in a position to alleviate the conditions which produce the negative feelings and consequences.

Job Attitudes and Satisfaction

In considering the possibilities for measuring individual adjustment, it is necessary to examine some of the other concepts currently interpreted as indicators of adjustment. In the literature on work, job attitude, satisfaction, and morale are commonly used interchangeably. Further, these are regarded implicitly or explicitly as essentially synonomous with personal adjustment in the work setting. For example, Herzberg, considering the implications of his job satisfaction research to mental health, states, "One could almost say by definition that a period during which one's attitude toward one's work is strongly positive is a period of good adjustment."[7] The relation between satisfaction and mental health is cited by Smith, Kendall, and Hulin (1969) as a primary rationale for their attempt to develop improved measures of job satisfaction.

Since job attitude is most often assessed by asking the individual to indicate his level of job satisfaction or dissatisfaction, this concept is most clearly related to our individual definition of personal adjustment. Thus, in stating that he is satisfied to some degree with either the global situation (e.g., his work in general), or with a specific aspect of his work (e.g., his supervisor), we may infer that the individual is subjectively assessing the degree of congruence between his requirements and his

---

[7]F. Herzberg et al., *Job Attitudes: Review of Research and Opinion* (Pittsburgh, Penn.: Psychological Service of Pittsburgh, 1957), p. 137.

realizations. Based upon this reasoning, good adjustment is reflected by satisfaction and poor adjustment by dissatisfaction. This analysis confirms that the common usage of job satisfaction as an indicator of adjustment appears justified when the *individual* definition is considered.

However, analysis of this concept in terms of our observer definition of adjustment is somewhat less straightforward. The crux of the increased complexity lies in the notion that there are multiple "parties at interest" who pass judgment upon the "goodness of adjustment" of the individual. That grossly different judgments may be made in this context can perhaps best be illustrated by a situation described by Argyris. Based on interviews with ten assembly-line workers who reported themselves satisfied with their pay, supervisors, and working conditions, Argyris derived the following list of characteristics of these workers:

1. They value money as most important. Seniority is second most important.
2. They all perceive themselves as having poor education.
3. They are unable to perform several different things at the same time (e.g., talk and use a screwdriver).
4. They aspire to do the minimum quantity of work, and do not feel badly about doing work that is of poor quality.
5. They tend to desire to be isolated and alone. They express no desire for group cohesiveness or "we feeling."
6. They are not loyal to the company and would leave to go to another job if they could be guaranteed a few cents more and retain their present seniority.
7. They are hardly ever late or absent from work.
8. They tend to dislike changes and are very rigid in their attitudes. They place a great deal of emphasis on prediction, ability, and security in life. Changes tend to threaten them.[8]

---

[8]C. Argyris, *Personality and Organization* (New York: Harper and Bros., 1957), p. 120.

These workers were judged to be adapted and adjusted (i.e., to have a good job attitude) by representatives of their employer. (We might infer that the workers would agree at least to some extent with this assessment since they reported themselves satisfied with several major aspects of their work situation.) Thus, in the judgment of the employer, certainly a viable "party at interest," there was an acceptable degree of congruence between the behavior of these men and the ascribed role requirements. Certainly Argyris, in company with a large group of behavioral scientists and organizational theorists, would not agree that these workers had attained an acceptable level of personal adjustment. Obviously, the differences between these judgments can be accounted for by the different role requirements used as criteria by the various parties at interest—the individual, the employer, and the organization theorist. This difference is important as a caution against equating job attitude or satisfaction with personal adjustment without first investigating the context of the data and determining which definition of adjustment is most pertinent.

The crucial issue here was discussed in part by Herzberg (1957) who differentiated between motivation seekers and hygiene seekers. After an intensive investigation of job attitudes, Herzberg proposed a two-factor theory in which job satisfaction and dissatisfaction are represented as separate continua rather than as opposite poles on a single continuum. Factors associated with a positive state of satisfaction are called motivator variables; those implicated in dissatisfaction are hygiene variables. The latter are primarily job context factors and function in the avoidance of discomfort, while the former are intrinsically job-related and are involved in self-actualization. If only hygiene variables are considered, the best outcome to be expected would be freedom from dissatisfaction.

Herzberg suggests that, based on their experiences in the work world, some individuals learn to react positively to the factors associated with the context of the job, i.e., become hygiene seekers. This state might be described as a generalized lowering of aspirations based on the realities of the work experience. The young man who sets out to conquer his world at 18 may, at 40, settle for an adequate paycheck and as short a work week as possible. These may well be the workers, described above by Argyris, who report themselves generally satisfied with their work. Here satisfaction may be more indicative of chronic apathy than the positive state usually labeled the same. The distinction between dissatisfaction and lack of satisfaction illustrates the distinction we have drawn between mental illness and personal adjustment. The latter implies more than freedom from symptomatology; it represents a dynamic equilibrium in all relevant aspects of the work area.

The implications of using job attitude as an indicator of personal adjustment level have been explored in the context of the individual and the observer definition of adjustment. Within the scope of the individual definition, the worker who reports himself satisfied indicates that his needs and realizations are fairly congruent. However, as pointed out earlier, the individual definition, while useful for theoretical discussion, is of limited use in the working world because the worker seldom functions alone. When other parties at interest are admitted, it becomes appropriate to repeat the question in the context of the observer definition of personal adjustment. That there are multiple persons and/or groups who claim an interest in the worker's adjustment is quite clear. It is equally clear that these individuals and/or groups may differ (perhaps quite radically) in their assessment of the worker's level of adjustment.

A production-oriented employer may look at his employee and make this assessment: He is well paid for his type of work; has a fairly comfortable work place (good lighting and ventilation); gets a two-week vacation each year; doesn't complain much; meets minimum production standards; and says he's satisfied with his job. Therefore, he certainly must be well adjusted. If Herzberg or Argyris were evaluating the same person they might consider the following factors in addition to those mentioned by the employer: The worker seldom has the opportunity to make a decision; has little control over his own work; has consistently lowered his level of aspiration through time; and has no long-range goals related to the job. Therefore, he must have a low level of personal adjustment because he is not fulfilling his potential as a human being.

Although these two parties at interest do not exhaust the possibilities, their positions indicate that it is always necessary to make a value judgment to assess individual adjustment from the outsiders' point of view. Is the worker well adjusted if he reports himself satisfied with his job and displays a job attitude acceptable to his employer? The answer must be: It depends.

Some Final Remarks

In this chapter we have highlighted the state-of-the-art in the measurement of personal adjustment. There are many criteria which have been investigated such as absenteeism, strikes, and sabotage. All of these criteria have economic consequences, and thus receive the attention of management. The results include absentee control programs which are coercive, insurance programs to provide hospitalization, and long-term binding labor contracts to reduce the frequency of strikes. While this approach *may* help management meet economic responsibilities, it is becoming quite clear that organizations are failing to meet their responsibilities to employees. That this strategy is no longer acceptable is clearly reflected in Federal legislation enacted during the past decade. If organization management will not lead in increasing the quality of life, they will be led.

Chapter 4

Organization Environmental Factors Affecting Individual Adjustment

THIS CHAPTER FOCUSES on personal adjustment within the limits of the business and industrial organization and, specifically, the identifiable characteristics of that environment. However, it should be noted that the work/personal life-space division is an arbitrary one because influences from all other areas of the individual's life space also affect his adjustment in the work environment. The influence of work-related variables upon adjustment outside the work situation has been called spillover by Kornhauser (1965). Iris and Barrett (1972) have suggested that the opposite relation also exists—that poor home adjustment may spill over and detrimentally affect personal adjustment on the job. Such spillover probably occurs in both directions, and is determined by both individual and environmental factors.

With this in mind, it should be profitable to discuss in some detail the organizational factors which seem to significantly influence an individual's adjustment in the work setting, and, less directly, in other areas of his life space.

The contact between the worker and the organization is multifaceted, and is comprised of both direct and indirect interfaces. These may be thought of as existing in a somewhat hierarchal arrangement. The worker is placed at the hub of a series of concentric circles with the more direct influences represented by the interior rings, and the more indirect influences, by the exterior rings. Although the direct and indirect levels interact interdependently, the latter may be expected to exert disproportionate influence upon the former. The guiding philosophy of the organization will limit the types of interaction possible at the other interfaces. For example, an organization in which employees are considered only as production units would probably have quite a different organizational climate from another in which the requirements of both men and equipment are considered in developing a balanced system. Obviously, the interactions among these various environmental variables as well as their impact upon the personal adjustment of the individual employee are exceedingly complex. To stay within the scope of the problem being considered here, we will limit our focus to the impact of organization environmental variables upon the worker's personal adjustment. Our proposed hierarchy of influence will be used as a guide for organizing this discussion, beginning with the broadest level of influence.

Management Philosophy

The guiding philosophy of the organization has an extensive impact upon all other organizational variables. Organizational goals are established at this level, and may vary from an exclusively profit-oriented philosophy to one incorporating economic and social criteria. The extreme profit-oriented company is exemplified by the old sweatshops where social responsibility was totally lacking and economic aims exclusively emphasized; a composite organization philosophy would incorporate economic and human values for organization members and/or society as a whole. Bass (1952) delineates three possible ultimate criteria of organizational worth: (1) the degree to which the organization is productive, profitable, and self-maintaining; (2) the degree to which it is of value to its members; and (3) the degree to which it and its members are of value to society. He suggests that the inclusion of the social criteria is axiomatic, and is based upon a value judgment consistent with the ideals of our democratic society. Although an organization must sustain itself, the personal adjustment of its members and its positive contribution to society are seen as intrinsically worthwhile goals.

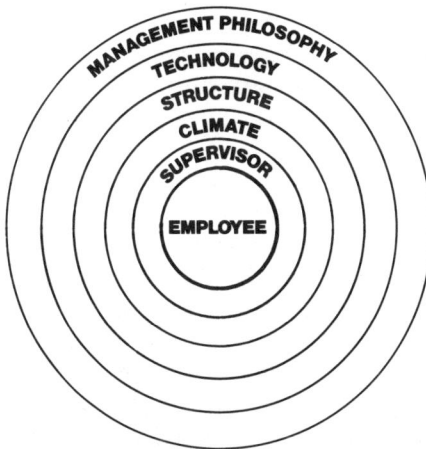

Figure 4.1: Organizational Influences on Adjustment

Our task here is to discuss the differential effects of management philosophies which represent acceptance of the various criteria. Since we're focusing on the individual in the work setting, we will consider only criteria 1 and 2. As Figure 4.1 suggests, management philosophy influences the individual indirectly through its impact on other organizational variables.

Argyris (1957) outlines the effects of the application of Taylor's (1911) classical management philosophy, which accepts only the production criterion, upon various aspects of the organization. Within this classical framework, a technological system is selected primarily for its efficiency in producing maximum capital returns for minimum expenditures. If the worker is considered at all, it is only for his physical capacities and limitations as a cog in the wheel of the production system. This orientation is represented by the time-and-motion study used to establish the relationship between the equipment and its operators. Conversely, when personal benefits to organization members are considered in addition to the economic critera, the resulting system is geared to produce psychological profits to its members as well as economic returns to the organization.

Classical management philosophy also calls for the organizational structure to conform to the principles of chain of command and span of control. The resulting structure is necessarily rigid, constraining, and cumbersome. However, it optimizes control of the system and all the components of the system including employees. The effects of control upon the individual will be reemphasized throughout the following sections. In contrast, when building a structure to meet the needs of organization members, the classical principles are deemphasized, and more consideration given to establishing good functional relationships among the individuals and groups who must cooperate to carry out the tasks of the organization.

The effects of management philosophy upon organization climate have not been specifically documented. Indeed, a set of climate dimensions, defined as workers' subjective impression of the work environment, has not been widely accepted by organizational researchers. Table 4.1 contains a sample of studies which identify the dimensions of organizational climate. Although there is some divergence among the results, there is also a considerable degree of overlap when the factors are examined across studies, suggesting that the various researchers are measuring something in common. In the absence of data on the relationship between management philosophy and organizational climate, we can only suggest that, on a subjective basis, it seems likely that the climate or atmosphere of a closely controlled, production-oriented organization would differ considerably from one having a more flexible structure and minimal rules and regulations. That climate does have implications for the personal adjustment of workers will be discussed in a later section.

While it may be theoretically possible for a supervisor to practice participative leadership in a production-oriented organization, such an individual would be the exception rather than the rule. The influence of the other organization variables clearly favors the authoritarian supervisor. The entire system rests upon the idea that control must be held by the upper levels of management and must be exercised rigidly. Therefore, the individual supervisor has little option but to dictate according to policy, even if he is inclined to behave differently. When, however, development of the capabilities of all employees and respect for the ability of each individual to perform and improve his own job are established as goals by management, the supervisor is encouraged to give responsibility and some decision-making power to his subordinates. Management encourages distribution of control so that each employee has a significant amount of responsibility for his own work. The supervisor then becomes a coordinator and planner of work rather than a driver of men.

TABLE 4.1 Expanded from Campbell, Dunnette, Lawler and Weick (1970).

Climate Dimensions	Author						
	Pace (1968)[1]	Litwin and Stringer (1968)[2]	Schneider and Bartlett (1968)[3]	Friedlander and Margulies (1968)[4]	Kahn, et al. (1964)[5]	Taguiri (1966)[6]	Litwin and Meyer (1968)[7]
Structure	Propriety	Structure and Constraint	Managerial Structure	Hindrance	Closeness of supervision	Practices re: setting of objectives, planning, feedback	Constraining conformity
Autonomy	Practicality	Emphasis on individual responsibility	Agent independence	Production emphasis	Rules orientation	Opportunities for exercising individual initiative	Responsibility
Reward Orientation		Reward and punishment; approval and disapproval	General Satisfaction	Consideration	Promotion-Achievement Orientation	Being without a profit-minded sales-oriented company	Rewards
Conflict	Awareness	Conflict and tolerance for conflict	Intra-agency conflict				
Standards	Scholarship	Performance and punishment; approval and disapproval		Thrust		Working without a superior who is highly competitive and competent	Standards

44

TABLE 4.1 continued

Consideration	Community Campus Morale	Organizational identity group loyalty	Managerial support; concern for new employees	Intimacy espirit aloofness	Nurturance of subordinates and universalism	Working of cooperative element people	Friendly team spirit
Miscellaneous	Quality of teaching and student-faculty relationships	Risk and risk taking		Disengagement			Organizational clarity

1. Pace, C.R. "The Measurement of College Environments." In *Organizational Climate: Exploration of a Concept*, edited by R. Tagiuri and G.H. Litwin. Boston: Division of Research, Graduate School of Business Administration, Harvard University, 1968.
2. Litwin, G., and Stringer, R. *Motivation and Organizational Climate*. Cambridge, Mass.: Harvard University Press, 1968.
3. Schneider, B., and Bartlett, C. "Individual Differences and Organizational Climate: I. The Research Plan and Questionnaire Development." *Personnel Psychology* 21(1968) 323–34.
4. Friedlander, F., and Margulies, N. "Multiple Impacts of Organizational Climate and Individual Value Systems upon Job Satisfaction. *Personnel Psychology* 22(1969): 171–83.
5. Kahn, R.L., Wolfe, D.M., Quinn, R.P., Snock, J.D., and Rosenthal, R.A. Organizational Stress: Studies in Role Conflict and Ambiguity. New York: Wiley and Sons, 1964.
6. Tagiuri, R., Comments on Organizational Climate. Paper presented at a conference on organizational climate, Foundation for Research on Human Behavior, Ann Arbor, 1966.
7. Meyer, H.H., "Achievement Motivation in Industrial Climates." In *Organizational Climate*, edited by R. Tagiuri, and G.H. Litwin. Boston: Division of Research, Graduate School of Business Administration, Harvard University, 1968.

We have broadly outlined two types of organizations having differing management philosophies and have indicated the influence of philosophy upon other organizational variables which affect the individual worker more directly. Next we will review the effects of these variables upon the personal adjustment of the worker.

Technology

Both the type and degree of technological development within an organization exert a major influence upon employees. As Broom and Selznik (1970) have pointed out, technology can be viewed as the environment within which the modern industrial worker lives. The emphasis here is again upon the pervasive influence of work-related variables in the worker's total life space. A sociotechnical system includes the specific technology of the organization, the formal division of labor, and the informal human relations within the organization. Often the technology determines, or at least limits, both the formal division of labor and the informal relationships which may develop within the organization. The rigidity of these limitations depends in large part upon the type of technology (e.g., craft, continuous process, assembly line), and the resulting effects upon individuals can be best examined by considering the major characteristics of each broad classification of technology.

In a continuous-process industry, employees have some freedom of movement and control of the technical apparatus. In addition, varying levels of skills are required so that employees have opportunities for advancement. While these conditions have not been established as directly contributing to personal adjustment, there is evidence to suggest that such a relationship does exist. Mann and Hoffman (1960) found that workers transferred into a completely automated power plant reported increased satisfaction with their jobs, and this increase seemed to derive, in part, from factors such as those mentioned above—increased freedom of movement and control of the equipment. Workers also felt that their skills were being utilized and that opportunity existed for increasing their level of skill.

The craft technologies permit the worker an even greater degree of involvement with his work than do the continuous-process technologies. In the former, the worker controls both the quantity and quality of his work, and is not limited to an isolated part of a product. This control allows the worker to produce a product with which he can identify. He can view the completed work with a sense of accomplishment, knowing that his abilities and effort are reflected in its quality. Craft workers also contribute both to the development of methods and the solution of problems within their area. All these factors combine to enhance the satisfaction of workers in the crafts. Broom and Selznick (1970) cite printing as an example of a craft technology. They report the results of a survey of factory workers in many industries which showed that only 36 percent of all printers would choose another occupation compared with 59 percent of all factory workers and 60 percent of automobile workers. Thus, as far as satisfaction with work reflects personal adjustment in the work setting, the craft technologies appear to contain a number of factors which contribute positively to the mental health of workers.

Although continuous-process and craft occupations utilize technological developments, the terms technology and automation are often associated with assembly-line systems. This application of technology on the assembly line has been the major subject of concern as to its negative effects upon the personal adjustment of workers. The inventions of such men as Eli Whitney and Henry Ford serve as landmarks in the trend toward fragmentation of work. The initiation of automated materials handling and standardized equipment provided the means by which this fragmentation became possible. Within the framework of early scientific management developed by Taylor (1911), emphasis was placed upon optimum utilization of money and materials while human needs were given little or no weight in the design of jobs or systems. To increase efficiency in producing a finished product, the total procedure was broken down into a series of simplified steps and each worker assigned to one facet of the work. The resulting assembly-line technology has the following characteristics (Broom and Selznik, 1970): speed of work and methods are predetermined; jobs are extremely specialized; little skill or training is required; there is little opportunity for advancement; and formation of informal work groups is inhibited. From a mechanistic point of view, these characteristics are quite well suited for accomplishing the goals of maximum production. However, this interpretation is based upon the assumption that the workers who are to perform the tasks are as standardized as the equipment with which they work.

Assembly-line work has often been linked to the alienation of the worker from the work process and thus to a condition judged as maladaptive by many contemporary social commentators. Alienation is described by Seeman (1959) as a state wherein the person experiences: (1) powerlessness—he is controlled and manipulated by others or by an impersonal system; (2) meaninglessness—his acts (i.e., work) seem to have no relation to his total life; (3) isolation—he feels alone in society; and (4) self-estrangement—activity is a means to an end, rather than an end in itself. Alienation and the conditions which initiate it are self-perpetuating—a vicious circle. The more the worker is used as a thing, the more likely he is to become alienated; and the more he exhibits the symptoms of alienation, the more likely he will be considered only a production commodity.

The automobile industry is often used as a prototype for the negative aspects of assembly-line work. Most automobile manufacturing plants are very large; the work is minutely subdivided and repetitive; most jobs require the same low level of skill; there is very little opportunity for advancement; and the worker never sees the finished product. The assembly-line operator takes his position at a continuous conveyor, knowing that he is interchangeable with hundreds of others in the plant. He never has the opportunity to experience closure on his job because the conveyor is a constant source of objects, each requiring the same predetermined response from him. Walker and Guest report a worker's comments which well illustrate this point:

> The assembly line is no place to work, I can tell you. There is nothing more discouraging than having a barrel beside you with 10,000 bolts in it and using them all up. Then you get a barrel with another 10,000 bolts, and you know every one of those 10,000 bolts has to be picked up and put in exactly the same place as the last 10,000 bolts.[9]

What, then, are the results of these conditions which prevail in the automobile industry? Blauner (1970) reports the results of a survey which show: 61 percent of automobile assembly-line (AAL) workers said their jobs were monotonous, compared with 38 percent of unskilled workers in the total sample of factory workers; 35 percent of AAL workers said their jobs were too simple to utilize their abilities, compared with 25 percent of the total sample; and AAL workers reported the greatest or close-to-the-greatest amount of dissatisfaction of all industries surveyed.

The results of Kornhauser's (1965) investigation of the mental health of automobile assembly-line workers are also illustrative of the condition described above. It was found that mental health varies directly with job level: workers with more highly skilled jobs tend to be better adjusted than those with unskilled jobs. For example, 56–58 percent of skilled and highly semiskilled

---

[9]C. A. Walker and R. H. Guest, *The Man on the Assembly Line* (Cambridge, Mass.: Harvard University Press, 1952), p. 54.

workers were found to have high mental health in comparison to 35-46 percent of ordinary semiskilled and 10-26 percent of repetitive semiskilled workers.

In attempting to assess the effects of different aspects of the various job levels as determinants of mental health, a number of variables were investigated. The factors found to contribute most heavily to level of adjustment were: the worker's feeling that the job does or does not give him a chance to use his abilities; and the perception of the job as interesting. These findings support the idea that alienation does exist among assembly-line workers, and that there is a negative relationship between this type of technology and personal adjustment.

To summarize, the effects of technology on individual personal adjustment seem to depend in large measure upon how the technological developments are utilized in designing a sociotechnical system. Those systems which allow the worker to develop and use skills, provide some opportunity for advancement, and allow the development of informal work groups provide a basis for the worker's good personal adjustment. Technology has a deleterious effect upon personal adjustment as direct function of the worker's being used as a thing or treated simply as a production commodity.

Organization Structure and Climate

After technological variables the set of factors which affect the individual worker includes organizational structure and climate. Both objective and subjective approaches are used to define these somewhat overlapping characteristics. Structure is defined objectively in terms of such factors as number of levels within the organization, size of subunits, total organization size, and shape of the organization. Table 4.2 (Ronan and Prien, 1971) compares results of some studies of organization structure with various other measures including employee performance and employee behavior. Integration of these results suggests that five factors can account for differences among organizations: standardization, centralization of authority, specialization, degree of technology, and organization size.Other factors appear to be unique to the separate studies and represent a composite of structure, climate, and behavioral measures.

In addition to Kornhauser's (1965) work which showed personal adjustment to be positively correlated with job level, Porter and Lawler report a series of studies relating these structural variables to job satisfaction. (As noted in Chapter Three job satisfaction is often used as an indicator of personal adjustment, but such an interpretation should be made cautiously.) Satisfaction was found to be higher in higher-level than in lower-level jobs (Porter, 1961); higher in smaller than in larger subunits (Porter, 1962); and complexly related to total organization size and shape (Porter and Lawler, 1965).

The more subjective concept of organizational climate is derived from the earlier work of Likert (1967) and Pace and Stern (1958) which stresses that only by assessing the individual's perceptions of his environment can relationships with end-result variables (in this case, personal adjustment) be established. In further developing the subjective view of climate, Tagiuri defined organizational climate as ". . . a relatively enduring quality of the internal environment of an organization that is: (a) experienced by its members, (b) influences their behavior, and (c) can be described in terms of the values of a particular set of characteristics (or attributes) of the organization."[10] While the data in Table 4.1 are assembled intuitively there appears to be considerable overlap with three of the dimensions appearing in the results of all seven studies. A total of only seven dimensions includes all results and suggests that employee perceptions can be parsimoniously described.

---

[10]R. Tagiuri, "The Concept of Organizational Climate," in *Organizational Climate,* eds. R. Tagiuri and G. H. Litwin (Boston, Mass.: Division of Research, Graduate School of Business Administration, Harvard University, 1968), p. 27.

Litwin and Stringer (1968) have attempted to develop a model which integrates the concept of organizational climate into a theory of organizational behavior. Using an instrument reflecting the climate dimensions listed in Table 4.1, they conducted a laboratory experiment to study the effects of variations in organizational climate. Three simulated business organizations were created using leadership style as the major variable input: the president of Company A emphasized the maintenance of a formal structure; Company B stressed friendly, cooperative behavior; and Company C placed high value on high productivity. Significant differences were found among all the dimensions of the climates thus created. Participants in two of the organizations (B and C) reported much higher satisfaction when structure and conflict were relatively low and responsibility, reward, warmth and support were high; low satisfaction occurred when the opposite set of conditions prevailed.

The main point of both Tables 4.1 and 4.2 is to illustrate the scope and nature of the work environment. Individual states and behaviors have been linked to both facets of the environment—structure and climate. However, this type of research is not abundant in spite of the convincing arguments that a link exists between the environment and the individual. Conclusive statements will require substantially more investigation than has been conducted.

Miller (1972) also investigated the relationship between organizational climate and job satisfaction using the Meyer (1968) climate questionnaire (see Table 4.1) and the job description index (Smith, Kendall, and Hulin, 1969). Each climate dimension was found to be important in determining satisfaction with at least one aspect of the job, and all aspects of the job contribute in some way to an idealized attitude of job satisfaction, although no valid means has yet been devised for calculating an index of general job satisfaction from the separate factor scores. So, although nothing definite can be said about mixtures of high and low satisfaction with the various job factors, the extremes can be discussed more confidently. The upper limit of general job satisfaction would be represented by high satisfaction in each of the areas of work, supervisors, coworkers, promotions, and pay. The organizational climate profile which was found most likely to produce these results would show elevated scores on the dimensions of responsibility, standards, reward, organizational clarity, and friendly team spirit, and a low score for constraining conformity. Descriptively, such a climate would include: a well-organized structure within which work could proceed smoothly, but with a minimum of unnecessary policies and procedures; a management which sets high standards for performance, gives the employee the freedom and responsibility necessary to carry out the job effectively, establishes a friendly and mutually trusting relationship with the employee, and provides equitable short- and long-term rewards in the form of recognition, encouragement, and promotions; and coworkers who contribute to the creation of an interpersonal atmosphere of trust and mutual support.

It appears likely that the concept of climate can be meaningfully included among the complex of organizational variables affecting the personal adjustment of the individual worker. Since climate appears to represent individuals' perceptions of many more objective aspects of the work environment, it has the potential for being particularly relevant for further study in personal adjustment.

Supervisor-Employee Interaction

The most direct level of interaction between the worker and the organization occurs in the supervisor-employee relationship. A number of models of this relationship have been proposed which describe both human and product-oriented approaches. McGregor (1960) notes that the underlying assumptions which a manager makes about the nature of workers determines the manner in

TABLE 4.2 Comparison of Studies of Results of Organization Structure, Performance, and Behavior

Pugh et al. (1968)	Prien and Ronan (1971)	Seashore and Yuchtman (1967)	Boyles, Eddy, and Frost (1963)	Palmer and Schroeder (1961)	Dunteman (1966)	Ronan and Prien (1973)
Structuring of activities	Standardization individual roles					
	Specialization				Technical personnel and control	
Concentration of authority						
Line control of workflow	Standardization individual recognition				Employee selectivity Pay-skill level	
					Retail sales personnel	
Relative size of support component						Degree of manufacturing
	Organization size	Business volume	Expansion of the work force	Size of work force	Size of organization	Unit size cost and salaried turnover
	Quality production	Production cost	Production efficiency			
	Marketing-tech. interface	Business mix	Contract production Company production		Allocations to labor vs product development	
		Manpower growth	Contraction of the work force		Work force reduction and job mechanization	Unit work force expansion and tardiness and insurance claims
	Change, products technology	Market penetration			Economic growth	

TABLE 4.2 continued

Marketing strategy			Job aversion	Tardiness vs family responsibility	Job withdrawal salaried Job withdrawal hourly
	Maintenance cost			Personnel tenure	Absenteeism Salaried turnover
	New member productivity			Community and employee support vs work output restriction	
	Member productivity	Grievance and job bids	Theft vs discounts	Authority—conflict behaviors (theft)	Unit ERI (Employee Relations Index)
Succession	Management emphasis		Cost of sickness vs use of machinery	Ownership and concern for organization interests	
	Youthfulness of members		Retirement welfare Thrift benefits Insurance benefits Cooperation with survey	Minority group Improvement of working conditions	

which he interacts with them. The Theory X manager assumes that people need authority and coercion to motivate them, and that they are lazy and will misuse any freedom allowed. The Theory Y manager makes very different assumptions: that people prefer to have control of their work, will seek and respond to challenges and responsibility, and that they can develop and grow.

Likert (1967) describes managerial styles in terms of four systems: (1) exploitative authoritative—use of authority and coercion with little regard for human needs; (2) benevolent authoritative—similar to 1, but paternalistic, attempts to buy workers with increased material benefits; (3) consultative—employees allowed to make suggestions and assist in planning, but management may be manipulative and also retains prerogative of accepting or rejecting suggestions; and (4) participative group—emphasis on talent and competence rather than authority as a basis for achieving organizational goals. The authoritative poles of the McGregor and the Likert models are examples of what has been called the authority-dependence relationship between supervisor and subordinate (Argyris, 1957). Argyris argues that this relationship is the logical outcome of the application of formal organization principles such as task specialization, chain of command, and span of control. Indeed, these principles are implicitly based on the same assumptions attributed to McGregor's Theory X manager and the authoritative systems described by Likert. They aim at subdividing work and the responsibility for planning and executing work so control is placed in the supervisor's hands, and he, in turn, is expected to closely watch a rather small group of subordinates.

Myers (1970) describes the same phenomenon in terms of the reductive use of authority. The system implies that the supervisor owns the subordinate; the social distance between the two is emphasized by such symbols as office size, special parking, dining facilities, and double standards concerning work-related behavior.

Argyris (1957) has also described the effects of the authority-dependence model upon the worker. Generally this system tends to make the individual dependent upon and passive toward the supervisor. Since he lacks control over his work and environment and does not have information necessary to predict the future, the worker's time perspective may be shortened. These two factors (dependence and lack of control) enter into a self-perpetuating cycle from which it is difficult to determine which factor is cause and which is effect. (The subjective selection of one or the other as the underlying cause of the phenomena may very well account for the differing sets of assumptions on the nature of the worker as described by McGregor.)

The earliest research relating leadership style to the behavior of group members were the Lewin, Lippitt, and White studies beginning in 1939. Adults serving as leaders of experimental boys' clubs took the roles of democratic or autocratic leaders. Marked differences between groups were found: with democratic leadership the groups were more cooperative, friendly, and constructive and valued their experience more highly; with autocratic leadership, members were more hostile to each other, less stable, and behaved disruptively if the leader were temporarily absent.

An experimental study reported by Strickland (1958) demonstrates the differential effects of close versus limited supervision. The situation was designed so that a supervisor was compelled to closely monitor the production of one employee while checking only occasionally a second employee performing identical work. The results indicated that supervisors came to perceive the monitored employee as untrustworthy and requiring close supervision, while the other worker was seen as trustworthy and capable of assuming responsibility for completing his job.

It seems then, that in the supervisor-employee relationship, the critical factor for adjustment is one common to the other interfaces described. This factor can probably be most clearly conceptualized in terms of control. The authoritarian supervisor is one who makes all the decisions, then instructs or orders his subordinates to perform the required work. Within this paradigm the employee has little or no control of his own actions. Considerable research attests to the negative outcomes of such an arrangement except under unusual conditions such as extreme danger or stress. Apathy, dissatisfaction, and even destructiveness have been shown to result from such coercive leadership. Control is clearly evident in the discussion of the effects of technology upon adjustment. Technology may contribute either positively or negatively to the worker's personal adjustment depending to a great extent upon whether he controls it, or it controls him. Similarly, in organizational structure and climate, satisfaction has declined with increasing inflexibility due to unwieldy size, cumbersome rules and regulations, or lack of individual responsibility, all of which detract from the worker's ability to control his work process effectively.

As was pointed out initially, little research has been directly and primarily concerned with individual adjustment. However, we have chosen those variables which have demonstrated relationships to personal adjustment criteria, and noted limitations where these exist.

Summary

In the chapter introduction we stressed that the worker is subject to a number of direct and indirect influences which interact to affect his personal adjustment in the work setting. Since the key concept in the relationship between the organization and the worker appears to be control, it should be considered in designing a sociotechnical system which balances human and production needs. A management philosophy which includes both social and production criteria for organizational success sets the stage for good personal adjustment of its individual members. In such an organization, a technological system should be designed or adapted to: (1) allow each worker a maximum amount of control over his own work; (2) divide work so that each worker can see some results of his labor; and (3) allow the formation of informal work groups to foster a sense of identity and loyalty to the larger organization. The organization structure should be designed to provide enough clarity that individuals and subgroups understand their relationship to other parts of the organization but are not hampered by excessive rules and levels of authority. Supervisors in such an organization should carry out their duties in a consultative rather than authoritative manner. Such an orientation includes a willingness to allow the employee to have a significant amount of responsibility for his own work and a voice in decisions affecting his job. The supervisor, then, becomes a source of help with problems, a planner and coordinator who links his group's output effectively with that of functionally related groups.

As defined earlier, climate is the subjective impression employees form based on the composite influence of all organization environmental variables. The climate of an ˙organization having the characteristics described above should reflect the employee orientation of the other variables within the limits of variations in individual perceptions. As such, it should approach the optimum condition outlined in Miller's (1972) research.

The questions which immediately arise are, "How can these optimum conditions be attained?" and "What can be done to improve personal adjustment in the absence of ideal conditions?" The following chapters attempt to answer these questions and to provide a positive plan of action to implement the suggested solutions.

Chapter 5

Constructive Intervention: The Mental Health Specialist

THE PREVIOUS CHAPTERS have focused upon the definition, criteria, and etiology of personal adjustment in the work setting. This analytical approach to mental health problems is an essential prerequisite to constructive intervention—the design and implementation of specific strategies to deal with personal adjustment failure. Based on the premise that personal adjustment is a function of the individual and the environment, it becomes appropriate to consider intervention strategies which emphasize the person or the situation or the interaction as the locus of adjustment failure. Strategies which involve intervention directed toward the person characterize the work of the mental health specialist.

Before defining the role of the mental health specialist in industry (and from this the treatment methods or approaches he uses), a historical account of the literature and significant events which have structured the field of occupational mental health may be helpful. The first full-time psychiatrist in industry was C. C. Burlingame (1946) who was employed by the Chency Silk Company in 1915. In 1919, the Engineering Foundation of New York asked E. E. Southard, director of the Boston Psychopathic Hospital and professor of neuropathology at Harvard, to investigate emotional problems among workers. Adopting a team approach which included the services of a psychologist and a social worker, Southard found that "62 percent of more than 4,000 cases reached the discharge status through traits of social incompetence rather than occupational incompetence."[11] This figure is still quoted today as a valid representation of a continuing industrial pattern.

The first "Review of Industrial Psychiatry" by Sherman (1927) appeared in the *American Journal of Psychiatry* and summarized the literature to that date. The author considered the "individual's adjustment to the situation as a whole" as the psychiatrist's rightful area of concern. Also, the psychiatrist was said to "attempt to forestall maladjustments by aiding in developing interests and incentives."[12] Until that time the stimulus for the development of industrial psychiatry could be traced to: (1) the work of industrial psychologists whose studies of abilities and intelligence were considered inadequate for investigating the total man; (2) the adjustment problems of men in the armed services during World War I; (3) the "propaganda efforts of the mental hygienists" including Southard; and (4) the introduction of scientific methodology into psychiatry.

Sherman concluded his first review of the field by

---

[11]E. E. Southard, "The Modern Specialist in Unrest: A Place for the Psychiatrist in Industry," *Mental Hygiene* 4 (1920).

[12]M. Sherman, "A Review of Industrial Psychiatry," *American Journal of Psychiatry* 83 (1927).

stating that the most successful method used in industrial psychiatry to aid the individual in readjusting to the industrial setting was one which endeavored to evaluate the total situation (or life space, in our terms), the worker's incentives and motivation as well as the immediate difficulties on the job. "Classification of maladjusted individuals into types or groups has been of little help."[13] Sherman suggested vocational counseling during the formative years to prevent many later industrial maladjustments.

The 1920s proved to be fruitful years in industrial psychiatry with more and more American industries and businesses employing full-time psychiatrists. The R. H. Macy department store introduced a mental health service in 1924. The now classic Hawthorne study began in 1927 at the Western Electric Company under the direction of Mayo and his associates (Mayo, 1933). The outcome of these studies indicated the enormous importance of human interactions as an integral part of the work situation.

The years following the depression evidenced a decrease in interest in the field with the notable exception of Mayo's continued research and Giberson's (1936, 1939, 1940) and Burling's (1939, 1942) maintenance of clinical activities.

Following World War II, many mental health specialists began focusing on specific problems such as psychosomatic reactions, alcoholism, accidents, the aging worker, the executive and his emotional problems, techniques of management education, and structure of the work environment. Unfortunately these professionals were more impressed with the mysticism of their cult than with demonstrating the practical efficacy of their intervention. While there are many narrative accounts describing problems and proposed solutions, few attempted to demonstrate the efficacy of therapy or of the preventive intervention.

---

[13]*Ibid.*

Beginning in 1955, a growing number of agencies such as the Menninger Foundation and the National Association for Mental Health have sponsored expanded training programs for psychiatrists, industrial physicians, and executives. Interest in industrial mental health was no longer confined to psychiatry and allied health professions, but extended to the popular press with articles in the *Wall Street Journal, Fortune,* and the *Saturday Evening Post.*

At present industry has initiated comprehensive programs including both part-time outside consultants and full-time staff personnel. Their work may be centered in the medical or personnel departments or the office of a senior executive. The work of these specialists may consist of standard clinical diagnostic evaluation and/or treatment with varying degrees of involvement in the actual work setting. Intervention may consist of clinical consultation, education, training, policy consultation, research, or a combination of these.

From this historical overview, it can be see that activity in industrial mental health has experienced a growth rate which parallels that of industry. Mental health specialists have expanded their services from simple clinical evaluations to include various treatments and input to organization management activities.

Labor's Approach to Mental Health Problems

In 1957 the National Institute of Labor Education was formed under the joint sponsorship of union leaders and mental health professionals. Its purpose was to stimulate research and develop programs in labor and mental health. A major stumbling block to such good intentions, however, was labor's insistence that any industrial mental health program must not be paternalistic if it were to be acceptable to labor. Also it could not be used to undermine the grievance process or to subvert union philosophy. Such cautions as these which were introduced in 1944 (Fountain, 1945) continue to influence labor's attitude towards industrial mental health projects. Consequently, there are few programs being launched under joint sponsorship.

Labor has been primarily concerned with providing programs rather than supporting research. It was not until 1959 that a specific clause, added to a collective bargaining agreement, provided funds for psychiatric care. Following this idea, accomplished by Retail Clerks Local 770 in Los Angeles, a number of other unions have negotiated contracts with similar provisions. The United Mine Workers of America, for example, contracted with a private mental health hospital in Virginia to serve their members and dependents through a program of traveling clinics. The demand for these services grew to such proportions that these clinics became permanent establishments in several communities, supported in part by fees collected from nonunion members. As can be seen from these programs, labor leaders are concerned about the personal adjustment of union members and are pressing for mental health services of a variety best suited to their particular needs. Generally this constitutes a first-aid approach, dealing with the problem after it has already produced serious consequences for the worker.

Constructive Intervention

Constructive intervention includes actions designed to: (1) prevent the occurrence of failure; (2) provide remediation at the time of failure (crisis intervention); or (3) facilitate recovery following failure. In recent years constructive intervention at these three stages has come to be identified as primary, secondary, and tertiary intervention. In the past, the mental health specialist relied *mainly* on tertiary intervention, an expensive approach of questionable effectiveness. Unfortunately, this is the model firmly embedded in professional training programs despite the obvious unfavorable cost-benefit status. On the other hand, primary intervention is not a one-on-one strategy, and is directed to all organization members prior to failure. The advantages of primary intervention in both human and economic terms have been touted for a decade, but practice lags far behind theory. While tertiary intervention leans heavily on the mysticism of psychotherapy, primary intervention depends on knowledge of the determinants of personal adjustment failure. Constructive intervention requires that we identify potential failure or those conditions which cause failure.

It is a truism that we can best learn where to go by learning where we are now. The mental health specialist can function in several roles: as an action agent practicing constructive intervention; as a multiplier extending his impact through other people he trains; or as a researcher providing the basis for action by other professionals.

Primary prevention in the orthopsychiatric model is a "community concept" (Caplan, 1964), the goal of which is to reduce the rate of new cases of adjustment failure in a specified target population. This is accomplished by identifying and consequently offsetting disruptive conditions before the detrimental effect occurs. Primary prevention views an individual as a representative of a larger group, and treatment is directed to causes of the problems of this larger group. While it is highly probable that some persons will experience adjustment failure, a program of primary prevention strives to reduce the incidence of failure. Finally, primary prevention is chiefly concerned with developing that course of action which will eliminate or minimize the undesirable situation in the future.

When viewed in the broadest possible perspective, the functions of mental health specialists in industry—whether psychiatrists, psychologists, or trained counselors—include a progressively expanding range of both clinical and preventive activities. The clinical services which have psychological and psychiatric implications for individuals can be listed as follows:

1. Appraisal of factors in the individual's personality which bear directly on his fitness or unfitness for work. This constitutes a part of both the employment interviewer's and the physician's preplacement examinations.

2. Recognition of neuropsychiatric conditions in their earliest manifestations, not only in applicants for work, but also as these conditions appear any time after employment.

3. Evaluation of neuropsychiatric factors in posttraumatic conditions covered by workmen's compensation laws.

4. Determination of the degree of employability or reemployability in postpsychotic states.

5. Consultation, when and where required, on the placement, transfer, promotion, or progress of individuals possessing valuable skills, but who exhibit potential personality handicaps or deviations in their interpersonal relationships.

6. Assessment of undesirable job behaviors such as absenteeism, tardiness, theft, sabotage, and so on.

7. Application of direct psychotherapy in selected individual cases as may be practical within the limits of the industrial setting.

If the industrial mental health specialist is to play an effective preventive role, he must widen his circle of influence beyond the confines of his medical department. This is not a new concept of the specialist's functions. In 1929 Dr. V. V. Anderson stated that the task of the mental health specialist in industry is not so much of providing clinical services for individual workers as it is to integrate his techniques with all personnel and supervisory procedures connected with the employment case history from inception to discharge.

How does one develop the role of the mental health specialist in industry? Any proposal for the extension and application of psychological and psychiatric knowledge and methods cannot be ordered or superimposed by force or by directives from the company's upper echelon. The mental health workers who represent psychology and psychiatry must initially gain the support of key people who are already engaged in human relations, personnel, medical, and labor relations work. One of the roles played by the mental health specialist is that of educator. Although times are changing, industry still views the mental health specialist primarily as a resource to deal with the obviously disturbed worker. It fails to recognize how this resource could also aid in maintaining the adjustment of nondisturbed workers or in increasing productivity of employees in work groups. Through effective presentation of these aspects of his profession, the mental health specialist is helping to dispel prejudices toward psychology and psychiatry as magic or witchcraft. One of the long-range benefits of this educational activity is change in management philosophy which may result in improved treatment of industrial workers. The continuous education and training of executives, foremen, personnel administrators, and labor leaders must emphasize understanding of worker behavior as it relates to personal adjustment.

Increased public sophistication results in increased demand for clinically trained specialists to extend their services beyond treating the emotionally disturbed. There is also a shift in interest from the therapeutic to the preventive, and a concomitant change in role from psychotherapist to consultant. Industry is beginning to utilize these new services to improve the overall well-being of workers and to increase organization efficiency. In addition, this shift to a consultative role may provide the opportunity to extend the impact of the professional by training nonprofessionals to perform a limited range of functions. The specialist here functions as a multiplier.

The future for the mental health specialist in industry appears favorable, provided he can demonstrate sufficient flexibility in a demanding and dynamic environment. Also he will be given considerable latitude to establish long-range programs and will have the opportunity to contribute to the solution of a wide variety of problems.

The mental health specialist in industry has numerous potential roles: preventer, implementer, therapist, mediator, researcher, educator. The development of the field depends on how he elects to manage these roles. If he chooses to narrow the definition of mental health specialist to that of psychotherapist or physician in time of emergency, then he severely limits his potential usefulness. The most fruitful approach is acceptance of all roles and competent fulfillment of their accompanying duties and demands. In this way the field of mental health can realize its potential to improve the worker's quality of life.

Chapter 6

Organization Development: A Limited Systems Approach

INDIVIDUAL INTERVENTION HAS been emphasized as the means of alleviating personal adjustment failures in the industrial setting. This is an apparent consequence of employing mental health specialists with that orientation in the industrial setting. Constructive action at the organization level is not so succinctly defined, however. Instead of being specialists in a limited field, organizational interventionists can be sophisticated industrial researchers or marginally trained personnel clerks. Strategies and methodologies range from the hardest engineering techniques to the subtlest psychological approaches. But despite these diversified, interdisciplinary sources, intervention at the organization level clearly has been dominated by the behavioral scientists working in conjunction with business managers.

Consistent with this relationship between behavioral science and business are the complementary assumptions that effective employees make effective organizations and that a well-adjusted, satisfied, and motivated individual is the most effective employee. These cherished, traditionally humanistic assumptions are reflected in most contemporary organizational theories (see, for example, McGregor, 1960; Argyris, 1970) and perhaps are valid. However, uncritical acceptance of intervention strategies arising from these assumptions has led many organizatins to consider (and often purchase at great expense) various programs designed to improve employee morale, increase management motivation, open channels of communication, and so on. Not only is there insufficient evidence endorsing any simple solution (such as packaged management training programs) to complex organizational problems, the little existing research only moderately supports even complex and carefully planned intervention strategies (Campbell et al., 1970). This lack of definitive evidence on the effectiveness of organization intervention strategies will receive further consideration shortly.

It would be a difficult if not fruitless task to review individually each organization's intervention strategies which might alleviate personal adjustment failures. One difficulty, implied above, is that elementary intervention strategies may be too restricted and self-limiting to be effective. Intervention limited to a single, isolated method such as a management training program which has been packaged for general consumption is a predictably ineffective tactic. Although changes frequently appear on attitude and opinion surveys following such training, these changes are invariably short lived, and their value in terms of improved managerial effectiveness is questionable.

The form of constructive intervention to be described in this chapter is a comprehensive rather than a restricted approach, characterized by broad diagnostic research, detailed planning, and various methods tailored to specific problems or conditions.

Organization Development Defined

Any attempt to describe traditional organization development (OD) depends on a small, productive school of organizational psychologists who have applied the philosophy first expressed by Douglas McGregor to actual work settings. Specific definitions reflecting this philosophy are offered by Bennis (1969), Beckhard (1969), French (1969), and Argyris (1970), but, in general, OD is viewed as a comprehensive, educative intervention strategy intended to increase organization effectiveness. Using material contributed primarily by McGregor and his students, Sherwood was able to arrive at a more elaborate consensual definition. In brief, Sherwood defined OD as (1) an educational strategy to bring about planned change; (2) based on an organizational diagnosis; (3) carried out by intervention; (4) within a complete, ongoing system; (5) to increase organization viability and effectiveness. Each of these characteristics requires elaboration.

First, OD is an educational strategy designed to bring about planned change within an organization. Specific strategies may vary widely (from sensitivity training to managerial grids), but the objective is usually the same: to change behavior through education with the implicit assumption that a change in attitudes, beliefs, or values precedes any change in behavior. However, this assumption is far from universally accepted. In fact, most researchers view the relationship between attitude and behavior as so complex that causality is not always discernible. There is evidence available to support the position that a change in attitudes may result in a change of behavior, but evidence also supports the opposite— that changes in attitude may result from behavior changes. Thus, when a consultant presents evidence of changing attitudes following a managerial T-group, is this change due to the group experience or to a memo from the president stating that "Things *will* be different after this management development program"?

While research on the effects of OD strategies is sparse, evidence suggests that something happens to participants' attitudes, even though it is not possible to conclude that behaviors change in a predictable manner. Thus, one might conclude that, considering the state of the art, organization change may be more haphazard than planners care to admit. For example, in a study on the effects of a T-group strategy, Underwood (1965) found that values and attitudes measured with a paper-pencil instrument changed significantly. However, the resultant behavioral changes were actually contrary to what the organization defined as effective performance. One positive note from this research was that an organization development program did result in organizational change, but the results also reiterate not only the complexity of the relationship between attitude and behavior but also the methodological difficulties of bringing about planned change through education.

A second characteristic of OD is that planning is based on a diagnosis of an organization or some part thereof. Argyris (1970) places great emphasis not only on initial organization diagnosis but also on continuous data collection and feedback which provides an ongoing diagnosis. This type of strategy is sometimes referred to as action research in which data are collected from individuals in the organization and then fed back to key personnel in the client system. At this point the interventionist engages in joint planning with those key personnel.

Familiar diagnostic methods include interviews, attitude surveys, and questionnaires which provide data that can be used to plan initial constructive action. Although this constructive action which can assume varied forms (such as selection or technical training), intervention, as the third characteristic of OD, is the principal mode of organization development.

Throughout this chapter intervention has been used almost synonomously with organization development. However, the term needs some clarification because many ways of intervening in an organization do not constitute organization development. Already mentioned, for example, are selection and technical training. Suppose a diagnosis suggests that high absenteeism among minority employees is a function of first-line supervision. One strategy might be to change selection procedures to place more competent individuals in the supervisory positions. An alternative or additional strategy might provide a general training program for supervisors. But to satisfy the definition of OD, a strategy or set of strategies must intervene in the organization's ongoing processes. Thus, in this situation, an OD strategy would probably focus on altering the attitudes and behaviors of the supervisors as well as the perceptions of the minority employees. A supervisor training program might be included, but only as part of a broader program in which specific skills are taught, transferred, and applied to the work setting. Thus, OD uses intervention which must be action-oriented to produce organizational change.

Intervention, in addition to interceding in the ongoing processes of an organization, also occurs at a system level. OD is planned for a total system or organization rather than for parts of a system. By definition it is never a piecemeal or patchwork effort designed to change a procedure here and to solve a problem there. Instead, organization development is designed to affect a total organization: to change (for example) a company's psychological environment or its management philosophy.

Although some purists interpret a total system to mean a complete company, many practitioners feel that any relatively autonomous subunit of a larger organization can be viewed as a total system. Thus, depending on the philosophy of the planners, an OD program might be initiated for a single work unit if the remainder of the organization had minimal influence and only general constraints on that unit.

The initial locus of intervention is a factor related to the systems approach to organization development. Much as the question of what constitutes a total system, the answer to the question of where does one start intervention depends largely on the planner's philosophy. Beckhard (1969), for example, feels that change must start with the organization's top man. If the organization is the total company, the top man would be the president or chairman of the board. Change in this organization, any change, would necessarily start with that person and proceed downward in the hierarchy. However, at the other extreme, Argyris (1971) states that effective intervention can be started at any level in the organization as long as it is in a relatively autonomous subpart of the organization. Neither extreme accurately reflects what determines the initial locus of intervention. Realistically, intervention begins where it is needed. In other words, the diagnostic stage which precedes planning and intervention will have a major influence on which company subparts must play a major role in the change process, which play a moderate role, and which may be safely ignored. Therefore, in some instances, the company's top man theoretically might not even be aware that a change program is in progress. More probably an organization development program would require not only his sanction but also his active participation. Beckhard's (1969) conclusions are fairly representative: if an OD effort is to be successful, at the very least the top management of the target system must be committed to the program and have a personal investment in its results.

The final dimension defining organization development is that it is intended to increase organization effectiveness. Just what constitutes organization effectiveness has not yet been agreed upon, but the characteristics of success which appear consistently in the literature (e.g., Bass, 1952; Georgopoulas and Tannenbaum, 1957; Georgopoulas et al., 1960) are flexibility and survival.

Thus Gardner (1965) and Beckhard (1969), for example, proposed sets of rules an organization must follow to be self-renewing or adaptable, their basic rationale being that a complex of economic, social, and psychological conditions is necessary for organization flexibility and continuity.

Objectives of OD

Because of its universal acceptance as the ultimate goal of any development effort, organization effectiveness was treated above as a basic property of OD. However, there are other common goals or objectives of OD which may vary according to specific organization problems; Sherwood (1971) lists several objectives which reflect common problems of organizations and correspond to a mental health focus. Among these objectives are the development of a viable, self-renewing system; the development of continuous feedback systems; the reduction of debilitating conflict; and the creation of an open, mutually trusting atmosphere throughout the organization. Additional objectives of OD might include increased awareness of interpersonal processes; reduced competition between interdependent subunits of the organization; or improved decision-making based on information sources rather than a particular role in the hierarchy.

The specific target groups—like the specific objectives—vary according to the problems or conditions requiring change. For example, if it becomes evident that change is advisable in managerial strategies, planning procedures, or cultural norms, the target group might be a specific management level. If change is needed to improve communication systems, increase work force motivation, or maximize intergroup cooperation, the target group might be a subunit within the organization.

Assumptions of OD

Although organization development can be defined and its major objectives specified, it is still an ambiguous concept. This ambiguity takes two forms: first, a considerable degree of the unknown remains about the specific effectiveness of OD despite increasing research; and second, OD is based on a set of abstract or inconclusive assumptions. Among these assumptions is the notion that the attitudes of most organization members toward their work are a function of their work environment rather than their personal characteristics. Thus, efforts to change work attitudes must be concerned with changing the environment or the individual's perception of the environment instead of the individual himself. Evidence supporting this assumption is available in recent organization structure research which finds organization size (Indik, 1965; Porter and Lawler, 1965) and job level (Porter and Lawler, 1965) related to both attitudes and behavior.

Another common assumption of OD is that most individuals desire responsibility and seek difficult tasks rather than avoid work. This, of course, is the basic premise of McGregor's Theory Y. A real problem exists with this assumption in practice because the actions of many managers are more consistent with the Theory X orientation toward subordinates. Thus, it is not uncommon to see the initial stages of an OD program directed at manager's basic attitudes on the nature of man and work.

Typical OD Strategies

Another means of describing and further defining organization development is to review intervention strategies typically associated with OD. Currently popular as general strategies, for example, are process consultation, Argyris's intervention model (1970), and the managerial grid technique originated by Blake and Mouton (1964).

As defined by Schein, process consultation is "a set of activities on the part of the consultant which helps the client to perceive, understand and act upon process events which occur in the client's environment."[15] In other words, a consultant provides insights to top management by analyzing the process of ongoing events. Schein further identifies six crucial processes the consultant is concerned with: communication, roles and functions of group members, group problem-solving and deductive strategies, group norms and growth, leadership and authority, and intergroup cooperation and competition. Thus, the process consultant analyzes the processes of ongoing events in the organization which may be related to its effectiveness, and then communicates his conclusions to the client. Depending upon his skills, the process consultant at this point may or may not become involved in the solutions of any problems he has identified, but typically he at least assists the client in finding possible solutions. Perhaps the unique aspect of process consultation is that it requires a certain degree of faith from the client since the consultant often will offer his services without a clear mission or need. That is, he does not have a specific program or plan of action. The client must accept the assumption, more or less on faith, that his organization probably could be more effective if the processes which need improvement were identified.

Argyris's (1970) model of intervention represents an integration of approaches often identified by action research. Research produces data which, in turn, are used to select an action or intervention strategy. Such action is then evaluated and the results are used to plan further action. Argyris presents a general, idealistic description of this model by identifying three basic requirements for any intervention strategy. First, an interventionist must be able to generate valid and useful information—a diagnostic process. Second, the client must be given alternative solutions by the interventionist to insure free and informed choice of action. Finally, to complete the requirements for effective intervention, the client must be

---

[15]Edgar H. Schein, *Process Consultation* (Reading, Mass.: Addison-Wesley, 1969), p. 9.

committed to the choice or decisions made. Although these three basic conditions apply to any type of consultative intervention (e.g., development of a selection program, job redesign, and so on), they are especially salient for OD planners who, by definition, must effectively intervene in an organization's ongoing process.

The third general strategy now popular is the managerial grid program developed by Blake and Mouton (1964), which employs a six-phase approach. First, the basic theoretical aspects of the grid are taught: how concern for the individual interacts with concern for production, producing a characteristic type of management. The next four phases of the program apply learned behavior principles to actual work or work-like settings. The final phase evaluates the first five phases and is used to establish new objectives. It should be noted that the grid approach, although general and flexible, is a specific program with many of the materials copyrighted by its originators.

In addition to more general intervention strategies, there are numerous specific techniques used with the general paradigms. These specific strategies include, among others, team building, intergroup problem solving, laboratory (T-group) training, confrontation meetings, and third-party consultation. With rare exception, the choice of strategies is determined by the preferences of the change agent or interventionist and, to a lesser degree, by the organization's requirements. In other words, individuals who attempt organization change tend to use strategies compatible with their philosophy and in which they are personally competent.

The Change Agent

Because organization development requires both the understanding and application of behavioral principles, it is not too surprising that a major source of change agents or interventionists is the behavioral sciences—especially psychology, sociology, and administrative or managerial sciences. However, behavioral scientists as consultants can often find themselves in an ethically compromising relationship with the client. For example, serious ethical implications may arise regarding a change agent's manipulation of individual organization members. Kelman (1965) mentioned the social scientist who was requested to study worker morale at an industrial plant. As a result of his diagnosis of the situation, his recommendations, and his intervening activities, management was able to employ techniques to improve morale. In this situation the interventionist might be criticized for helping management achieve its goals at the individual worker's expense. Kelman further notes that the underlying assumption is that "the worker is being manipulated so that he experiences a sense of participation and involvement that is not reflected in the reality of his position in the industrial organization."[16] In a pragmatic sense, if such manipulation and tinkering with workers' perceptions designed to favor management are discovered, it is possible to achieve outcomes that are opposite from stated OD goals. Instead of reduced conflict or a "self-renewing system," an interventionist's inappropriate manipulation of individuals can result in distrust and defensiveness.

A final issue is that the change agent's locus in the system may be either internal or external. In a consultative capacity, an external interventionist may be necessary to effect any significant change in the organization. In addition to being less contaminated by personal involvement with the system, he often has extensive experience in similar situations and can use his aura or personal impact as a professional to great advantage.

---

[16]Herbert C. Kelman, "Manipulation of Human Behavior: An Ethical Dilemma for the Social Scientist," *Journal of Social Issues* 21 (1965): 1.

Although the internal change agent may have certain advantages such as intimate knowledge of the system, being a part of the system can have a distorting influence. Also, internal change agents are often relatively powerless in the system (e.g., personnel people) when compared to the external change agent who typically enters the system with the active support of top management. A somewhat different position is held by Bennis (1969), who feels that the external-internal issue is academic after the early phases of an OD program have been completed. Any advantages an external agent might have become less a factor as the program develops and the agent's aura fades.

Conclusions

One now might ask, "What does organization development have to do with mental health, specifically?" The answer is in a fundamental assumption: what are called instances of poor personal adjustment are to a great extent products of psychologically destructive environments. An organization can develop a psychological environment which is not only incompatible with employees, but also may contribute to their psychological failures. Thus, organization development—as one model of change—attempts to create (using education) a more compatible environment for employees, an environment that will not only minimize personal failures, but one that will also stimulate personal motivation, effort, and growth.

Treating OD as a model for environmental change is a rather theoretical rationale for linking OD to mental health. From a pragmatic point of view the link is somewhat more difficult to make, however. For example, "Just what constitutes a *compatible* environment?" and "What are the specific, critical aspects of the environment which affect behavior or result in poor personal adjustment?" are questions which remain unanswered for the practitioner as well as the theorist. Certainly this lack of understanding—a total absence of causal information—contributes significantly to the disappointing research findings on OD effectiveness. Perhaps organization development will continue to provide greater promise than results until a time when more basic questions about behavior in organizations can be answered.

An alternative explanation for the mediocre results of OD programs is that organization development is restricted by its focus on the human element alone. The next chapter will explore a somewhat different intervention approach in which there is a dual focus: the individual and his technological environment.

Chapter 7

Sociotechnical Intervention

IN THE PRECEDING chapters attention was focused first on intervention at the individual level, then at the organization level. These approaches, focusing on either the individual or the organizational element exclusively, constitute half solutions and, according to the available evidence, appear to have marginal benefits at best.

Individual-level interventions—counseling or psychotherapy—are necessary to deal with crises, but do not solve the basic organizational problems. We recognize that some individuals will fail seriously, and as a result may have a profound and detrimental effect on the organization. Individual-oriented remedial action is definitely required for these crises. However, discomfort or failings short of crisis proportion are far more widespread and constructive intervention requires intervention which will touch *all* those in need.

85

At the organization level, conventional OD practice focuses primarily on human relations with the assumption that personal failings in industry stem primarily from faulty interpersonal relations. On the other hand, the sociotechnical approach assumes, at its core, that technical change has a profound effect upon social relations and that planning, change, and remediation must take this interaction into account (Woodward, 1965). Trist (in Bennis, 1969) states that this approach to organization development recognizes the "open system" quality of organizations and attempts to "relate the social *and* technological systems to each other."[17] Therefore, the major difference between the sociotechnical and OD models is that the former recognizes and deals with both the human aspect and the man-machine aspect of the total system. Man-machine system is a generic description which includes both the conventional man-machine interface of the production-line industrial worker *and* the less conventional interface of the clerical and managerial worker. More accurate terms should be used to describe the characteristics of jobs within any particular setting. Each individual, regardless of job functions, performs that job *embedded* in a unique setting. Since neglect of this point has resulted in the many negative consequences discussed in previous chapters, the sociotechnical alternative then seems to hold promise not found in the OD model. In essence, sociotechnical intervention includes consideration of those factors which are the focus of conventional OD intervention. However, the target of intervention are the factors which affect relations rather than the relationship per se.

When placed into a historical context, it appears that the sociotechnical approach to organization development is a logical step in industry's attempt to advance its

---

[17]E. L. Trist, "On Socio-technical Systems," Chapt 6.1 in W. G. Bennes, K. D. Benne, and R. Chen, eds., *The Planning of Change* (New York: Holt, Rinehart, and Winston, 1969).

applied technology. Singleton (in Warr, 1971) notes that the past two centuries have seen an emphasis placed upon technical advances. Having met with almost unqualified success, this undertaking has created some new problems. Some aspects of technological advance have taxed the capacity or limitations of the industrial worker, and attention has now turned to this man-machine interface.

Within the United States, the sociotechnical approach first appeared in the 1930s, but the real impetus to employ this approach to job design and organization development came with World War II when psychologists were called upon for applied work in developing man-machine systems. To discuss the present stage of development of this approach in terms of a theoretical model is difficult. To some extent, the absence of such a model reflects the newness of the field but more so the lack of organization and the paucity of both research and theory.

Despite the absence of a universal model, it is possible to overview past research to give a general idea of the relationship between main variables as defined by existing research findings. Given additional research, the relationships among the main variables will undoubtedly become clearer. At present it is difficult to say with certainty what leads to what. This intelligence is particularly important for the design of intervention strategies. For example, if the objective of intervention is to improve worker morale then we must know what factors *cause* poor morale.

Poor personal adjustment has definite implications for the organization at large. To the degree that an individual is maladjusted his general functioning is *suboptimal.* Recognition of this fact is not likely to come from a production-oriented approach to organization design which at most infers such inner states in terms of economic outcomes. Under these circumstances the organization subjugates the individual's needs to the system, ignoring him until he deviates from the established norms. At this point, the deviation is corrected or the individual is released from the organization.

Techniques of Intervention

At present, the sociotechnical system is an abstraction and as such it is not a predictive tool (Woodward, 1965). Woodward notes that the sociotechnical approach serves as a basis for "speculative thinking" as opposed to a "guide to action."

One implication is that all of the standard approaches to research and evaluation may be employed within sociotechnical studies as long as the end results are viewed in light of the complex man-machine interface of the particular situation. Study may be at any level, from the individual to the entire organization. However, when viewing an organization as a whole, one must view optimization of production in its effect on the roles and interaction of the individuals involved, the explicit understanding being that social events do affect the objective organizational goals of production.

Without going into detail, most of the sociotechnical research already performed fits neatly into the scheme required by the scientific method. Generally an independent variable has been identified which involves some manipulatable aspect of the organizational environment (e.g., line vs. bench work, and so on). The manipulation of a particular variable usually reflects a desire to implement some technological change with the goal of increased output and/or quality of production. To continue an experimental task, relevant dependent variables are measured to determine the effect of the manipulation. Such variables seem to fall into two general categories. The first of these might be labeled global behavioral changes which result from an experimental manipulation. At a glance, such measures as quality and quantity of production, turnover, absenteeism, tardiness, damage, and so on, seem to reflect organizational interest in a change.

The second set of dependent variables might be referred to as the personal-individual response to change such as workers' level of satisfaction, feelings of isolation, anomie, and so on. As will become apparent later, these two classes of dependent variables are related to one another.

Research: Outcomes, Consequences, and Implications

Using this scientific approach to investigate the effect of change upon a sociotechnical system, there are several possible means of obtaining data. One technique is to obtain baseline measures of relevant dependent variables under preexisting organizational conditions. These baseline measures serve as points of comparison for measures following organizational change. If one does not wish to risk change without evidence of success, or if several alternatives are being considered, equivalent subgroups can be exposed to different conditions, with the resulting changes being compared to one another and to the baseline measures.

Thus, in the past, research and theoretical development within the sociotechnical approach has been oriented toward a particular aspect of a single man-machine system. The objective in any single study is usually determined by the investigator's personal interests and the opportunity to solve the organization's problems.

The practical question now concerns the focus of sociotechnical intervention. The key to this dilemma lies in the identification of organization conditions and job characteristics which are related to desired outcomes. In any particular setting then, initial research must identify the conditions and characteristics which have a causal relation to the target outcomes. For example, if the target outcomes are product quality and less absenteeism, the prescription for intervention requires identification of the causes of quality work and absenteeism. If the researcher is lucky, his efforts yield an answer *and* the basis for intervention.

To continue the example, suppose absenteeism has been linked to the supervisor/subordinate ratio and that supervisors with larger numbers of subordinates have high rates of absenteeism. At this descriptive level, two intervention prescriptions are available. First, more supervisors could be hired and second, the need for supervision could be reduced. If the research probes even further, the nature of the link may be understood. Perhaps it is not a matter of numbers alone but the fact that a larger number of subordinates leads to increased job specialization where each worker has his own elemental task to perform. This finding leads to an alternate prescription—to cross-train workers or to delegate authority downward to reduce the need for supervision. Again, if the researcher is lucky, quality of work will be similarly linked to its causes which will provide the basis for further intervention.

The point here is that there is no cut-and-dried prescription for sociotechnical intervention. There is some evidence for about eight organization conditions and about six job characteristics which can be considered determinants (causes) of organization and individual effectiveness (Price, 1968). However, these are abstractions (e.g., centralization of authority as an organization condition and degree of worker control as a job characteristic) and have unique form and substance in each setting. What is actually done to change degree of worker control for a clerical job will be very different from what is done to change a welder's job. This uniqueness is in itself an obstacle to formulating principles or guidelines for sociotechnical intervention.

Research into the Effects of Sociotechnical Intervention

One place where an individual worker comes in direct contact with an organization is the task to which he has been assigned. Following the industrial revolution, the average worker's role has become considerably more routine and repetitious. Study has shown that the production advantage gained by mechanization may involve some unpredicted negative side-effects. Walker and Guest (1952) indicate that mechanical pacing of work seems to be directly related to turnover and absenteeism and inversely related to morale.

To investigate one particular parameter of routine work, Whyte (1955) performed a study in which operators who spray painted toys were allowed to individually regulate the speed of the conveyors which carried the finished toys to the next operation. This was in contrast to the prior condition in which the conveyors moved at the same speed for all operators (i.e., paced vs. nonpaced conditions). Within three weeks, work output under the new condition was 30–50 percent above the expected level. However, unpredictable consequences arose from this change in production method. Finished products came off the line too quickly for the next department to handle, and the painting line simultaneously was ahead of the unit which supplied them with toys to paint. To end this disruption, the department returned to the original mode of operation. Before leaving this study, it is worth noting that the change of work conditions which was investigated was suggested and agreed upon by the workers themselves. Such group participation in decision-making will be discussed as a variable in its own right.

Davis (1966) reports another study in which an organization employing a paced assembly line tested two experimental job designs. One was called the group job design, in which individual workers rotated among stations without any pacing of work. In the second, or individual job design, each worker obtained his own materials, performing all operations including the final inspection. In the group job design, production dropped by 11 percent but quality, measured by percentage of defective pieces, improved. The individual job design, however, resulted in a slight increase in production and a relatively sharp increase in quality. Perhaps it is worth noting Davis's comment that "Pacing eliminated responsibility for productivity, and job rotation, with the grouping of work stations for identical operations, practically eliminated individual responsibility for quality of work performed."[18] If one were to forward a purely economic theory of motivation, it would be difficult to explain these findings. The workers seemed to respond positively to increased responsibility rather than shy away from it.

Another set of variables which affects the functioning of the individual worker involves such organizational aspects as division of labor and mechanization. These features of an organization cannot be discussed independently because they seem to be related to each other as well as to other variables such as paced work. Despite this inability to extract or differentiate the influences of these variables, some research has been performed which has disclosed workers' responses to the qualitatively different environments produced by these variables. For example, Davis (1966) reports a series of four experiments, in radically different organizations, which sought to determine the effects of division of labor and mechanization. The quality common to the four situations was that the workers' tasks were highly specialized, repetitive, required no skill, and involved no visible finished product. Davis demonstrated that when workers could perform multiple functions, be a part of a unified group, have a meaningful field within which to work, and be able to feel some accomplishment with the completion of a product unit, there tended to be an in-

---

[18]L. E. Davis, "The Design of Jobs," *Industrial Relations* 6 (1966): 28.

crease in worker satisfaction, output efficiency, and quality.

One disadvantage which seems to accompany the division of labor is the increased likelihood of conflict within work groups (March and Simon, 1959). The suggested cause is that competition arises and individual goals (being first) become more important than group goals (production). However, competition between groups does not seem to be a major problem associated with division of labor. Price (1968) notes that the effectiveness of mechanized systems can be lost due to the workers' dislike of the conditions created by mechanization, which is expressed in absenteeism, tardiness, and job withdrawal.

When the division of labor is low, the grouping of workers does not seem to have detrimental effects. Instead, mutually supportive roles allow both the work and any resulting stress to be shared by the workers, eventually producing group roles which the individuals acknowledge and accept. This, of course, is not possible where there is a high division of labor and the individual worker must face the job and its accompanying stress without any group support.

Given the diverse findings presented, what guidelines can be inferred? Unfortunately, as Woodward (1966) has stated, "the same principles can produce different results in different circumstances" and, therefore, any rules obtained through research are very limited as a guide to action.

Two general conclusions have been drawn from this body of research. First, job redesign *tends* to result in an increase in the quality of production rather than the quantity critical to organization interests. Also, satisfaction improves and absenteeism decreases, both critical outcomes in the organization. The second finding seems to be that managers making decisions about organizational structure need to know more than just the technological requirements of the situation (Woodward, 1967). While this appears to be eminently supported by the research, what type of background, i.e., training, experience, ability, and so on, is best suited to such an undertaking?

In the final analysis, the sociotechnical approach to organization change views the system as open and dynamic. As such, any aspect of it may be manipulated to further human and/or organizational goals. In fact, Trist (in Bennis, 1969) notes that attempts to develop such systems need not be concerned only with internal functions but may deal with extra-organization factors, e.g., developing new markets, changing old ones, and so on. The warning generally attached to the manipulation of any part of such a system is that repercussions of the change may be felt, which are unpredictable in their place and form of manifestation. This, however, does not suggest a policy of avoiding change but merely points out the necessity for comprehensive evaluation of any change which is undertaken.

The sociotechnical approach is valuable for its inherent quality of being a system of checks and balances. It attempts to maximize organization efficiency while, at the same time, adds to the assurance that the individuals involved are being subjected to those conditions which are most compatible with their functioning as human beings. Checks and balances imply that the adjustment of the individuals within a work situation is not an independent factor, but one which interacts with all aspects of the organization, an indication that a sacrifice of one factor for another will, in the long run, be detrimental. This fact alone—even without consideration of the worker as an individual striving for adjustment—should motivate all involved to develop a total system most compatible with the needs, capacities, and capabilities of the individuals who populate the system.

How does adjustment, using our definition, play a role in this system? The answer to this lies within the concept and definition of adjustment. As people interact with a particular environment they *care* to adapt to it. At times, however, this adaptation may be necessary and at the expense of personal or individual adjustment. When viewed by others—peers or supervisors—a person performing adequately at work may be deemed normal or adjusted. This inference is highly inappropriate since it neglects the individual's emotional-intellectual state. Rather than using adequate work performance as a criterion, adjustment is more realistically based upon the individual's perception of his work being compatible with his needs, interests, and so on.

As discussed previously, manifestations of serious maladjustment are most obvious and quite widespread, including everything from lateness to sabotage and feigned illness to actual physiological damage as a result of stress. Given these extreme examples, both personal maladjustment and its disadvantage to the organization are quite obvious. What has not received explicit recognition, however, is that lesser degrees of maladjustment (e.g., dissatisfaction, feelings of isolation, powerlessness, and so on) also produce undesirable consequences. Although they are of a lesser magnitude, such consequences involve a wide range of antiproductive and nonproductive behaviors. Whether this has been overlooked in the past or intentionally ignored due to the difficulty involved in correction is not known. However, the problem now faced by industry is that the effects of maladjustment on the work environment have grown to a proportion difficult to ignore. Whether one chooses to view this situation from a moral-ethical standpoint (i.e., a person spends one-quarter of his life on the job and he should not be subjected to conditions unfavorable to his development and functioning as a human being) or from a pragmatic viewpoint (i.e., conditions which workers find to be dissatisfying ultimately lead to some decrement in productivity and, therefore, should be changed), the conclusions reached are virtually identical. If industry is to continue to grow, it must invest time and money on self-evaluation,with the expressed intent of reorganizing and redesigning the man-machine system so that the interface allows a person to be both a productive worker and a well-functioning individual.

Chapter 8

Mental Health in Organizations: Values and Priorities

WHILE WE CANNOT provide uncontested comparisons with historical data, it does appear that the incidence of adjustment failure in organizations is increasing. Certainly the statistical indices of organizational behaviors which we have used as criteria of adjustment have changed. Absenteeism appears to be increasing, turnover is as high as ever, and the incidence of overt conflict—strikes— continues at an alarmingly high level. While alternate and mutually exclusive explanations may account for the statistics, the fact remains that the lot of the individual is not what it could be. The statistics of economic affluence in America are deceptive: while the industrial worker eats, has shelter and *some* security, we contend that he is psychologically malnourished. Work conditions for the majority are such that more is extracted from the individual than is returned to him. The individual is an element in a system designed to optimize economic efficiency with little consideration for personal, social, and psychological consequences.

This book's main thesis is that things can be different. The individual's quality of life can be substantially improved through the intelligent use of psychological and sociotechnical intervention to produce innovative solutions. Some evidence does exist to support this thesis, but it has gone unnoticed and unused by industrial management. While it would be convenient to conclude that industrial management is at fault for its ignorance of potential constructive actions, the evidence also suggests that the social and behavioral scientist must share the responsibility. Specifically, the typical researcher is not action-oriented, and, although he communicates with his fellow professionals, he does not communicate with those individuals who are in positions to implement constructive action programs. While there are hundreds of highly competent and sophisticated researchers active in industrial-organizational research, the typical industrial executive is familiar with a mere handful, and is *perhaps* knowledgeable about the work and position of only one or two. This coupling problem plagues the technical product and process-oriented research and development scientist. The transfer of results from the laboratory or from the scientific journals to the shop floor is not an autonomous process. The transfer and implementation must be managed if they are to be accomplished at all effectively.

In the absence of effective coupling of personal adjustment research and management practice, we can hardly expect to find innovative management of human resources. Instead, managers must rely on their own common sense, and adapt to the priorities with which they are presented. The manager is expected to conduct the operation of the enterprise to produce an economic profit, and to the extent necessary, to maintain the human organization. We use the term maintain purposely since it describes the objective of the typical personnel or industrial relations effort—custodial maintenance.

Maintenance through the use of pacifiers may alleviate some symptoms, but the basic problems remain unsolved. For the majority of individuals these pacifiers constitute Herzberg's (1957) hygiene solutions, particularly those which can be assimilated into the workers' off-the-job life such as holidays, vacation time, shorter work weeks, and so on. Incomes provide workers with sufficient surplus to buy the boat, the recreation equipment, the cars, and the time to alleviate the effects of detrimental work conditions. An unknown but substantial majority of the working population has *learned* to accept this compensation, and has thus conceded to the destructive, dehumanizing nature of their work. Only a minority look to and engage in these diversionary activities for supplemental satisfaction, adding to an already satisfying and meaningful work experience. Until recently labor itself reinforced this approach to management through contract demands for pacifiers. Increases in wages and salaries and benefits such as insurance and retirement policies can be expressed unambiguously. However, recognition, opportunity based on merit and psychological meaningfulness of work are difficult, if not impossible, to express clearly as contract demands. And if expressed, the means to enforce compliance simply do not exist. What is necessary, then, is a comprehensive and diligent effort from managers to develop and to implement innovative and creative management.

The type of innovative management and the potential alternatives described in Chapters Six and Seven can produce work which is meaningful, satisfying, and motivating. When these conditions exist, work can constitute an enriching experience which adds to, rather than detracts from, the individual's psychological well-being. The evidence, however meager, to support this position is remarkably convincing. Some of the applications of conventional organization development action programs and the less conventional sociotechnical innovation have produced significant economic and social results. Specifically, sociotechnical intervention has demonstrated that production either remains constant or drops slightly but temporarily while quality improves over former levels, and most important, the incidence of negative mental health criteria declines. Absenteeism, conflict, job attitudes, and satisfaction show marked improvement. What then are the deterrents to more widespread application of these apparently potent techniques of constructive intervention?

Resistance to change is typically considered a phenomenon associated with rank-and-file employees. However, this phenomenon can and does occur throughout the organization hierarchy. Application of the techniques described requires a substantial change on the part of all organization employees and particularly those who have primary responsibility for operating the enterprise.

Two types of changes are required. First, and probably most important, there must be a change in values to rank the personal and social consequences of work equal to its economic consequences. Once this is accomplished (not a minor task), the alternative technical and managerial skills and actions must be understood and mastered. Given both changes, the owners of the organization must be willing to accept the expense of change, if there is a cost. Manufacturing plants are designed to operate in a specific way (such as a continuous assembly-line operation); redesign of the work and specific jobs may make major portions of the physical plant obsolete. A good example of this is the much publicized Vega plant in Lordstown, Ohio. The deterioration in labor-management relations and the subsequent strike during 1972 was accompanied by vociferous complaints of meaningless jobs, repetitiveness, machine-paced work, and so on, all of which are characteristic of the highly mechanized assembly operation. The employee-sponsored solution in this setting followed the example of the Swedish Volvo assembly plant in which work teams assembled an entire unit. This approach, first implemented in the Volvo truck plant, at least initially has been accompanied by *no decrease* in productivity and a *marked decrease* in employee absenteeism (absenteeism was one of the serious problems in the Vega plant). Based on the experience in the truck plant, in 1972 Volvo designed a new automobile assembly plant to accommodate the team work organization.

Other deterrents to constructive action are many and varied, and often are embedded in our culture. Change through constructive action must be accomplished within the existing organization structure with minimal destruction of the productive capability of the organization. Destructive change is unacceptable, although some temporary loss of efficiency may be required during the process of change. It is quite possible that the cost incurred as a result of this transition may never be recovered economically. However, the improved quality of life is important, and thus can become a justifiable organization objective. The idea that organizations are responsible to the public and to their employees in more than economic terms is not new (Bass, 1952), although it has not been very popular. Recent developments in Federal legislation incorporate a broader view of organization responsibilities. Implementation of these concepts, though, remains at the organizational level and there is yet little evidence that management is focusing on the job of the individual. Reports in the public press suggest that innovations in some form (usually job redesign or participative management) have been undertaken in seventy or more organizations employing a total of 10,000 workers. Other estimates triple or quadruple those figures, but whatever the multiplier this represents an insignificant percentage of the current *millions of* American workers.

What is to be expected in the future, during the decade of the 70s and beyond? In this time of change, and as we approach the leisure age, the current concepts and definitions of work do not seem to be defensible and are, perhaps, ultimately self-defeating. What does appear to be a defensible concept of work for contemporary and future uses involves economic, personal, and social criteria. What constitutes work, then, is a conglomerate of physical, mental, and emotional responses of the individual directly or indirectly related not only to total economic and social system goals but, additionally, to the goals of the worker himself. The definition of work must be relevant to the total individual, not his economic utility alone. Changes in the conduct of enterprise are being demanded and as the possibility of an improved quality of life becomes common knowledge, the demands will become increasingly difficult to satisfy with sham solutions or pacifiers.

The crucial changes will have to focus on the relation of individual wants and needs to his experience. Research reports substantial agreement among employees at different levels in the organization hierarchy on the importance of the work performed, the importance of their job-contribution to company products, promotion, and fair pay as the general bases for job satisfaction.

The concept of work and the characteristics of work performance which yield recognition must be defined to include some dignity and meaning in the wide variety of occupations and activities essential to the achievement of the good life for everyone. To achieve some reasonable compromise with the future we must give up some of our most cherished values, a change of the most basic kind in the value structure of our society. If we are to survive in a manner no worse and perhaps better than today, then we must change as a society.

Progress in making work fit for humanity will require answers to several basic questions:

1. What are the salient characteristics of and conditions of work from the individual's perspective? A massive amount of research data, both complementary and contradictory, exists, *claiming* to specify the factors which affect the status and behaviors of employees. Ade-

quate tests of these hypothesized factors have not been done other than on a pilot research basis. The critical research remains to be done.

2. What are the methods and requirements for making work a beneficial, humanly enriching experience? This is the test to validate the salient factors hypothesized above. The question, though, concerns *how* we intervene. Job redesign, participative management, or human relations training for supervisors are proposed, but they are empty phrases until research demonstrates *why* application of these methods *cause* the desired outcomes. Continued blind, shotgun approaches to problem-solving are unacceptable.

3. What are realistic and appropriate individual, organizational, and national goals? The assumption has been voiced that some proportion of jobs will always be unattractive, unfulfilling, and/or aversive, and that this is a necessary condition of competitive enterprise. A utopian existence or even its approximation is not a human right according to some; it is an earned privilege.

4. What are the obstacles to progressing toward a rational personnel management, and how are these obstacles to be overcome? In view of the promising research and application of the job design-enrichment paradigm, why are so very few applications attempted? Is greed the compelling motive of owners and managers and is altruistic humanity a figment of the imagination?

We are certain that the key problems have not been exhausted, that there are many questions which must be answered before we can be assured that the social and behavioral sciences have fulfilled their obligation to man and society. Until the professionals and entrepreneurs jointly attempt to improve the quality of life of the worker, many now dormant questions will remain unasked and unrecognized. Only comprehensive action/research will lead to progress.

Attempts to solve the problems suggested here obviously demand a multidisciplinary research approach and action. Most of all, active participation *and* sponsorship of those individuals capable of contributing solutions are required; patchwork will no longer suffice. To continue to allow inadequate concepts of the past to dictate the future is to show ignorance of the collision course of our system.

While the concepts presented here are likely to be regarded as utopian, we believe that changes in our culture are coming either on a voluntary or involuntary basis. Levels of education, availability of information, and the pressure for individual recognition are increasing. The relative quality of life accepted or tolerated by past generations of workers is today unacceptable. The aspirations and expectations of contemporary workers are logical, and will require an unprecedented level of excellence in management.

Bibliography

Argyris, C. *Intervention Theory and Method: A Behavioral Science View.* Reading, Mass.: Addison-Wesley, 1970.

_____.*Management and Organizational Development.* New York: McGraw-Hill, 1971.

_____.*Personality and Organization.* New York: Harper and Bros., 1957.

Astin, A. "Criterion Centered Research." *Educational and Psychological Measurement* 24(1964): 807–22.

Barker, R. *Ecological Psychology.* Stanford, Calif.: Stanford University Press, 1968.

Barrett, G. V. *Motivation in Industry.* Cleveland: Howard Allen, 1966.

Bass, B. M. "The Ultimate Criteria of Organization Worth." *Personnel Psychology* 5(1952): 157–73.

Beckhard, Richard. *Organization Development: Strategies and Models.* Reading, Mass.: Addison-Wesley, 1969.

Bennis, W. G. "Changing Organizations." *Journal of Applied Behavioral Science* 2(1966): 247–63.

_____.*Organization Development: Its Nature, Origins, and Prospects.* Reading, Mass.: Addison-Wesley, 1969.

Berdie, R. F. "A University Is a Many-Faceted Thing." *Personnel and Guidance Journal* 45(1967): 768–75.

Blake, R. R. and Mouton, J. S. *The Managerial Grid.* Houston: Gulf Publishing Co., 1964.

Blauner, R. "Social Alienation." In *Automation, Alienation and Anomie,* edited by S. Marcson. New York: Harper and Row, 1970.

Boyles, B. B., Eddy, W. B., and Frost, C. F. Organization Data and Multivariate Analysis. Chicago paper, MPA Convention, 1963.

Brayfield, A. H. "Human Effectiveness." *American Psychologist* 20(1965): 645-57.

Broom, L. and Selznik, P. "Technology and Human Behavior." In *Automation, Alienation and Anomie,* edited by S. Marcson. New York: Harper and Row, 1970.

Burling, T. "Personality and the Economic Situation." *American Journal of Orthopsychiatry* 9(1939): 616-22.

_____."The Role of the Professionally Trained Mental Hygienist in Business." *American Journal of Orthopsychiatry* 11(1942): 48.

Burlingame, C. C. "Psychiatry in Industry." *American Journal of Psychiatry* 103 (1946): 549-53.

Campbell, J. P., Dunnette, M.D., Lawler, E. E., III. and Weick, K. E., Jr. *Managerial Behavior, Performance, and Effectiveness.* New York: McGraw-Hill, 1970.

Caplan, G. *Principles of Preventative Psychiatry.* Basic Books Inc.: New York, 1964.

Cronbach, L. J. *Essentials of Psychological Testing.* 3rd ed. New York: Harper and Row, 1970.

Davis, L. E. "The Design of Jobs." *Industrial Relations* 6(1966): 21-45.

Dollard, J. and Miller, N. E. *Personality and Psychotherapy.* New York:McGraw-Hill, 1950.

Dunteman, G. H. "Organization Conditions and Behavior in 235 Industrial Manufacturing Organizations." *Journal of Applied Psychology* 50(1966): 300–305.

Forehand, G. A., and Gilmer, B. Von H. "Environmental Variation in Studies of Organizational Behavior." *Psychological Bulletin* 67 (1964): 361–82.

Fountain, C. W. "Labor's Place in an Industrial Mental Health Program." *Mental Hygiene* 29(1945): 95.

Fredrickson, N. "Toward a Taxonomy of Situations." *American Psychologist* 27(1972):114–23.

French, J. R. P. "A Theory of Status and Health." In *Mental Health and the Work Environment.* Report of a seminar sponsored by the Foundation for Research on Human Behavior and the National Institute of Mental Health, edited by Sven Lundstedt, 1962: 31–45.

French, W. L. "Organization Development Objectives, Assumptions, and Strategies." *California Management Review* 12 (1969).

Fulton, W. J. "Industrial Medicine Potentials: A Time and Job Analysis of Medicine in Industry." *Journal of Industrial Medicine,* 1949.

Gardner, W. "How to Prevent Organizational Dry Rot." *Harper's,* 1965.

Georgopoulas, B. S., Indik, B. P., and Seashore, S. *Some Models of Organizational Effectiveness.* Ann Arbor, Mich.: Institute for Social Research, University of Michigan, 1960.

Georgopoulas, B. S. and Tannenbaum, A. S. "A Study of Organizational Effectiveness." *American Sociological Review* 22(1957): 534–40.

Giberson, L. G. "Psychiatry in Industry." *Personnel Journal* 15(1936): 91–95.

_____."Emotional First-aid Stations." *Personnel Journal* 16(1939): 1–15.

_____. "Pitfalls in Industry for the Psychiatrist." *Medical Women's Journal* 47(1940): 144-46.

Glatter, A. N. "Criteria of Adjustment." *American Psychologist* 12(1957): 748-49.

Habbe, S. "Management's Changing Views on Alcoholism." *The Conference Board Record* 5(1968): 49-52.

Herzberg, F. *Work and the Nature of Man.* Cleveland: World Publishing, 1966.

Herzberg F., Mausner, B., Peterson, R. O., and Capwell, D. *Job Attitudes: Review of Research and Opinion.* Pittsburgh, Penn.: Psychological Service of Pittsburgh, 1957.

Herzberg, F., Mausner, B., and Snyderman, B. *The Motivation to Work.* 2nd ed. New York: Wiley, 1959.

Hoppock, R. "Criteria of Adjustment." *American Psychologist* 12(1957): 232.

Indik, B. *Three Studies of Organizational and Individual Dimensions of Organizations.* Technical Report No. 15, ONR, Contract No. NR-404(10), May 1965.

Iris, B. and Barrett, G. V. "Some Relations Between Job and Life Satisfaction and Job Importance." *Journal of Applied Psychology* 56(1972): 301-4.

Kasl, S. N. and French, J. P. "The Effects of Occupational Status on Physical Mental Health." *Journal of Social Issues* 18(1962): 67-89.

Kelly, E. L. "Consistency of the Adult Personality." *American Psychologist* 10(1955): 659-81.

Kelman, H. C. "Manipulation of Human Behavior: An Ethical Dilemma for the Social Scientist." *Journal of Social Issues* 21(1965): 31-46.

Kornhauser, S. *Mental Health of the Industrial Worker.* New York: John Wiley and Sons, 1965.

Lanyon, I. S. "Mental Health Technology." *American Psychologist* 26(1971):1071-1076.

Levinson, H. *Emotional Health in the World of Work.* New York: Harper and Row, 1964.

Levinson, H., Price, C. R., Munden, K. J., Mandle, H. J., and Solley, C. M. *Men, Management, and Mental Health.* Cambridge, Mass.: Harvard University Press, 1966.

Lewin, K., Lippitt, R., and White, R. K. "Patterns of Aggressive Behavior in Experimentally Created Social Climates." *Journal of Social Psychology* 10(1939): 271-301.

Likert, R. *New Patterns of Management.* New York: McGraw-Hill, 1961.

_____. *The Human Organization.* New York: McGraw-Hill, 1967.

Litwin, G. H. and Stringer, R. A., Jr. *Motivation and Organizational Climate.* Boston: Division of Research, Graduate School of Business Administration, Harvard University, 1968.

Mann, F. C., and Hoffman, L. R. *Automation and the Worker: A Study of Social Changes in Power Plants.* New York: Henry Holt, 1960.

March, J. G. and Simon, H. A. *Organizations.* New York: John Wiley and Sons, 1959.

Mayo, E. *The Human Problems of an Industrial Civilization.* New York: Macmillan, 1933.

McGregor, D. *The Human Side of Enterprise.* New York: McGraw-Hill, 1960.

Menninger, W. C., and Levinson, H. "Industrial Mental Health: Some Observations and Trends." *Menninger Quarterly* 8 (Fall 1954):1-13.

Meyer, H. H. "Achievement Motivation and Industrial Climates." In *Organizational Climate,* edited by R. Tagiuri and G. H. Litwin. Boston: Division of Research, Graduate School of Business Administration, Harvard University, 1968.

Miller, L. M. "Job Satisfaction as a Function of Individual Need Gratification and Organization Climate." Master's thesis, Memphis State University, 1972.

Mischel, W. "Continuity and Change in Personality." *American Psychologist* 24 (1969), 11, 1012–18.

Myers, M. S. *Every Employee a Manager.* New York: McGraw-Hill, 1970.

Pace, C. R. and Stern, G. C. "An Approach to the Measurement of Psychological Characteristics of College Environments." *Journal of Educational Psychology* 49(1958): 269–77.

Palmer, G. and Schroeder, R. H. "Incentive Conditions and Behavior in 188 Industrial Manufacturing Organizations." Technical Report No. 3, Office of Naval Research, Contract No. NR–475 (08). June, 1951.

Peak, H. "Attitude and Motivation." In *Nebraska Symposium on Motivation,* edited by Marshall Jones. Lincoln, Nebr.: University of Nebraska Press, 1955.

Pervin, L. A. "Performance and Satisfaction as an Individual-Environment Fit." *Psychological Bulletin* 69(1968): 59–68.

Porter L. W. "A Study of Perceived Need Satisfaction in Bottom and Middle Management Jobs." *Journal of Applied Psychology* 45(1961): 1–10.

_____. "Job Attitudes in Management: I. Perceived Deficiencies in Need Fulfillment as a Function of Job Level." *Journal of Applied Psychology* 46(1962): 375–84.

Porter, L. W. and Lawler, E. E., III. "Properties of Organizational Structure in Relation to Job Attitudes and Job Behavior." *Psychological Bulletin* 64(1965): 23–51.

Price, J. L. *Organizational Effectiveness—An Inventory of Propositions.* Homewood, Ill.: Richard D. Irwin, Inc., 1968.

Prien, E. P. and Ronan, W. W. "An Analysis of Organization Characteristics." *Organizational Behavior and Human Performance* 6(1971): 215–34.

Pugh, D. S., Hickson, D. J., Henings, C. R. and Turner, C. "Dimensions of Organization Structure." *Administrative Science Quarterly* 13(1968): 65–105.

Roethlisberger, F. J., and Dickinson, W. J. *Management and the Worker.* Cambridge, Mass.: Harvard University Press, 1943.

Ronan W. W. and Prien, E. P. "An Analysis of Organizational Behavior and Organizational Performance." *Organizational Behavior and Performance* 9(1973): 78–99.

Schein, E. H. *Process Consultation.* Reading, Mass.: Addison-Wesley, 1969.

Seashore, S. and Yuchtman, E. "Factorial Analysis of Organizational Performance." *Administrative Science Quarterly* 12(1967): 377–95.

Seeman, M. "On the Meaning of Alienation." *American Sociological Review* 24(1959): 783.

Sells, S. B. "Dimension of Stimulus Situations Which Account for Behavior Variance." In *Stimulus Determinants of Behavior,* edited by S. B. Sells. New York: Ronald Press, 1963. Pp. 3–15.

Serrin, W. "The Assembly Line." *Atlantic* 228(1971): 62–73.

Sheppard, H. L. *Industrial Society: The Emergence of the Human Problems of Automation.* New York: The Free Press of Glencoe, 1955.

Sherman, M. "A Review of Industrial Psychiatry." *American Journal of Psychiatry* 83(1927): 701–10.

Sherwood, J. J. "An Introduction to Organization Development." *Experimental Publication System* 11(1971): No. 396–1.

Singleton, J. W. and Drutz, A. "Interface: Man and Machine: Two Scientists Look Ahead." *Perspectives in Defense Management* June(1969): 27–35.

Singleton, W. T. *Introduction to Ergonomics.* Geneva World Health Organization, 1970.

Smith, P. C., Kendall, L. M. and Hulin, C. L. *The Measurement of Satisfaction in Work and Retirement.* Chicago: Rand McNally and Co., 1969.

Southard, E. E. "The Modern Specialist in Unrest: A Place for the Psychiatrist in Industry." *Mental Hygiene*4(1920):50.

Strickland, L. H. "Surveillance and Trust." *Journal of Personality* 26(1958): 200-15.

Tagiuri, R. "The Concept of Organizational Climate." In *Organizational Climate,* edited by R. Tagiuri and G. H. Litwin. Cambridge, Mass.: Division of Research, Graduate School of Business Administration, Harvard University, 1968.

Tan, G. "A Study of Personal Adjustment in the Work Setting." Masters thesis, Memphis State University, 1972.

Tannenbaum, A. S. "Personality Change as a Result of an Experimental Change of Environment Condition." *Journal of Abnormal and Social Psychology* (1957):404-6.

_____. "Control in Organization: Adjustment and Organization Performance." *Administrative Science Quarterly* 7(1962): 236-57.

Taylor, F. W. *The Principles of Scientific Management.* New York: Harper and Bros., 1911.

Trist, E. L. "On Socio-Technical Systems." Chapter 6.1 in *The Planning of Change,*edited by W. G. Bennis, K. D. Benne, and R. Chin. New York: Holt, Rinehart and Winston, Inc., 1969.

Underwood, W. J. "Evaluation of Laboratory Method Training." *Training Directors Journal* 19(1965): 34-40.

Vroom, V. H. *Work and Motivation.* New York: John Wiley and Sons, 1964.

Walker, C. A. and Guest, R. H. *The Man on the Assembly Line.* Cambridge, Mass.: Harvard University Press, 1952.

Warr, Peter B. (Ed.), *Psychology at Work.* Baltimore: Penguin Books, 1971.

White, R. W. "Motivation Reconsidered: The Concept of Competence." *Psychological Review* 66(1959): 297–333.

Whyte, W. F. *Money and Motivation.* New York: Harper and Bros., 1955.

Woodward, J. *Industrial Organization: Theory and Practice.* New York: Oxford University Press, 1965.

Work in America. Cambridge, Mass.: The MIT Press, n.d.

Zeitlin, L. R. "A Little Larceny Can Do a Lot for Employee Morale." *Psychology Today* 5(1971): 22 ff.

Index